"Dr. Norvene Vest's radical call for reform in *Claiming Your Voice: Speaking Truth to Power* names many complex levels of our culture, but perhaps is most urgent in the political landscape. Her exposé will not settle for simply patching once again a sinking ship with the band-aids of greedy, self-serving and economic bromides. She insists we entertain 'a prophetic imagination' to move us into a political theology of caring and serving the larger community— so to heal de-formations through compassionate re-formations. Anything less imprisons us in the same bloated, exhausted 'empire'; instead of continuing 'following the profits,' we must choose instead following the prophets."

> — Dennis Patrick Slattery, Ph.D. Distinguished Professor Emeritus in the Mythological Studies Program at Pacifica Graduate Institute and author of *The Way of Myth: Stories' Subtle Wisdom*

"In an age when some lament the absence of public theology, Norvene Vest's *Claiming Your Voice* is a welcome and timely articulation of an important role for religion and spirituality in social discourse. Readers will find its combination of the Hebrew prophetic tradition and the Benedictine wisdom tradition refreshing and thought-provoking."

> — Cyprian Consiglio, OSB Cam, Prior at New Camaldoli Hermitage, Big Sur

"Vest challenges us to put on our mature Christian 'pants' in order to face into the hard truths of our times. By speaking the truth in love, she invites us to center ourselves in the Holy Spirit while moving to bring about the change our communities and the world yearns for. The community renewal she urges will require deep listening, faithful prayer, acceptance of our human limits and courageous hope. This is a brave voice speaking to those who wish to be courageous Christians in the work of transformation."

> — Bishop Diana Akiyama, Episcopal Diocese of Oregon

"*Claiming Your Voice* is an urgent appeal to heed for our times. Rooted in timeless Benedictine wisdom and the Old Testament prophetic tradition, Norvene Vest exposes us to the sobering realities we all confront in our world today and issues a challenge for us to elevate such witness into active public engagement that allows the 'sacred' to permeate our common life. A hugely provocative yet hopeful read!"

> — Wil Hernandez, PhD, Obl OSB, spiritual director, author, and executive director of CenterQuest

Claiming Your Voice

Speaking Truth to Power

Norvene Vest, Obl OSB

LITURGICAL PRESS
Collegeville, Minnesota

www.litpress.org

Cover design by John Vineyard.

Scripture quotations are from New Revised Standard Version Bible © 1989 National Council of the Churches of Christ in the United States of America. Used by permission. All rights reserved worldwide.

© 2022 by Norvene Vest
Published by Liturgical Press, Collegeville, Minnesota. All rights reserved. No part of this book may be used or reproduced in any manner whatsoever, except brief quotations in reviews, without written permission of Liturgical Press, Saint John's Abbey, PO Box 7500, Collegeville, MN 56321-7500. Printed in the United States of America.

1	2	3	4	5	6	7	8	9

Library of Congress Cataloging-in-Publication Data

Names: Vest, Norvene, author.
Title: Claiming your voice : speaking truth to power / Norvene Vest, Obl OSB.
Description: Collegeville : Liturgical Press, 2022. | Includes bibliographical references. | Summary: "Vest examines four contemporary de-forming patterns-market culture, American empire, climate crisis, and racism-and describes the strengths that Benedictine spirituality and prophetic imagination offer to energize and bring healing to public life"— Provided by publisher.
Identifiers: LCCN 2022010132 (print) | LCCN 2022010133 (ebook) | ISBN 9780814667934 (paperback) | ISBN 9780814667941 (epub) | ISBN 9780814667941 (pdf)
Subjects: LCSH: Catholics—Political activity—United States. | Christianity and culture—United States. | Christianity and politics—United States | Christianity and politics—Catholic Church. | Church and state--United States | Churchand state—Catholic Church. | Benedictines—Spiritual life. | Christian life—Catholic authors. | BISAC: RELIGION / Christian Living / Social Issues | RELIGION / Religion, Politics & State
Classification: LCC BX1407.P63 V47 2022 (print) | LCC BX1407.P63 (ebook) | DDC 261.7088/28273—dc23/eng/20220401
LC record available at https://lccn.loc.gov/2022010132
LC ebook record available at https://lccn.loc.gov/2022010133

*To the many Benedictine monastic
women and men who have been so generous
with their hospitality and ideas to me,
I am infinitely grateful.*

Contents

Section III
Formative Challenge to Public Policies

Preface

Many years ago, I read an essay by German economist and sociologist Max Weber called "Politics as Vocation," or in German, *Politik als Beruf*. I confess I was more fascinated by the title than by the content.[1] I knew that the German "beruf," like the English word "vocation," had religious overtones. I knew also that the English word "politics" had its roots in the Latin "polis," referring to public life in community, the common realm. Then, as now, I was fascinated both with faith and with public/political life, and thus intrigued by the idea that one could have a political calling similar to a religious calling. Today, I am aware of how urgently each of us, as a member of American public life, is called to bring our faith in a God of grace and surprise into the public arena, not as an ideological demand but as a commitment to engage the presence of the sacred here and now. This book is a summons to that work.

I deliberately use the term "sacred" because it is not limited to one denomination, one political party, or to single issue politics. On the other hand, it does imply a consciousness of and commitment to the active presence of the holy in our midst. In the twenty-first century, many views of God coexist side by side, even among people of avowedly common faith. As a progressive lay Episcopal Christian woman and a Benedictine oblate, my own faith has deep roots and fluid boundaries. I understand the sacred not as something wholly transcendent and separate from the material world, but as embedded within all of creation. So, when I advocate for the sacred in public life, I refer to the presence of that elusive reality within and among us, ever oriented toward compassion, justice, and the well-being of all. Sometimes, like a misguided lover, we attempt to treat various idols as holy, until eventually we are called up short. Such attempts end sooner or later in tragedy. But for now, I am suggesting the necessity of many citizen voices raised alongside expert and political considerations—voices that speak beyond the limitations of the moment in favor of what I call the common good. Rapid advances both in technology and global communication make it increasingly urgent that we find ways to invite and imagine the active presence of a just and merciful God in our public policy deliberations.

The First Amendment of the American Constitution prohibits any specific religious institution from imposing its ideology on our common life, but both the founding documents of our country and common aspirations of many religions urge and encourage public commitments to compassion and justice for all. Nevertheless, the public arena today in the United States tends to be quite intentionally secular, and while the practice of personal religion is allowed, it has been largely treated as marginal and inappropriate in the public arena.[2]

Yet, somewhat to the surprise of commentators, religion remains vital for many residents of the US. Ideally, politics and theology would engage in a mutual, creative interplay that strengthens each to be open and willing to be modified for the sake of real charity in the present moment, a possibility explored in the emerging term "political theology." Although the state can no longer see itself as entirely secular, no new language or self-understanding has yet been developed to guide a thoughtful and fruitful integration of the sacred in public life.

My guess is that many of us have a suspicion that our faith ought to affect all the dimensions of our lives. But we may be wary of the sharp (and sometimes false) clarity of some Christian involvement in politics because we sense that religious beliefs do not typically translate immediately and simply into political behavior. We might hope to find ways to make ourselves intelligible to our neighbors in terms of our religious commitments but are wary of public engagement too tightly tied to precise political agendas or expressed in intolerant fashion about issues that may seem civically imprudent and/or theologically impious. As a Christian woman and oblate of a Benedictine monastery, I myself have often written about faith, but seldom tried to speak to its possible role in public policy.

In particular, it is sometimes alleged that Benedictine Christians, monastic or lay, are committed to withdrawal from the dangerous temptations of the world.[3] Some Christians do not view engagement with "the world" as an unqualified good, thinking that worldly "temptations" may be too powerful for a faith-filled person to avoid. I am convinced, however, that the Rule of St. Benedict[4] (which, of course, is based on the Christian Gospel and other religious books) is a useful spiritual guide not only for monastics but also for the common life, because the Rule makes clear that valuable opportunities for spiritual work lie precisely in noticing and amending our faults as revealed in our daily relationships with others and within our communities.

As a Benedictine oblate (a lay person committed to engage the Gospel as informed by Benedict's Rule) I also find the Rule (in Latina called *Regula*, meaning not a demand but rather a sort of measuring stick) to be a very helpful resource in integrating the sacred in public and common life. And so Benedictine spirituality is the first foundation that undergirds this book, as a practical resource for witness and challenge to distorted public policies.

As attested in the first paragraph, my personal story and this book are grounded not only in Benedictine spirituality, but also in a love and respect for public/political life. At the beginning of my work life, I joined President Lyndon Johnson's "Great Society" program, working in the Department of Housing and Urban Development to provide housing for lower income families and senior citizens. In retrospect, I see that service was a way to express my desire to work for justice, even while isolated from worship. I loved doing that work for fifteen years, but gradually became aware that our housing programs often benefitted the banks and the builders more than the families and elderly in need. And gradually I sensed that for me, justice work was unfulfilling absent a sense of God's presence guiding it.

After those years in the field of public policy, I went to seminary, earned a degree in theology, and began a ministry of writing, teaching, and spiritual direction, finding sacred grounding in affiliation with a local Benedictine monastery and membership in a vital, progressive Episcopalian community. Over the thirty-plus years that have followed, I have been privileged to hold deep conversations with a variety of persons seeking to make God's Spirit a real and guiding presence in their lives.

With this movement, I also realized a return to my previous undergraduate and graduate studies in political theory, recognizing anew the close relationship of political theory and theology in the long-ago days when Plato and Aristotle struggled with fundamental questions of human life: What is life for? How do we live together in community? What are virtue and wisdom, and how are they gained? Central to my earliest, conscious self-understanding was the Greek ideal of the *polis*, literally meaning the city or city-state. As the Greeks understood it, the *polis* offered a vision of life in which people belong to one another and have learned the virtues of living together as community. As we now know, Greek city-states did not live up to their ideal, excluding, among others, women and slaves from public life as well as squabbling with one another over power. But the ideal itself lasted for centuries, notably bearing a close resemblance to the ideal of community in Judeo-Christian and Benedictine life.

The second foundation that recurs throughout this book is borrowed from the practice of prophecy, particularly as found in the Old Testament. I sense that human life within any society is subject to critique. Retired Archbishop of Canterbury the Rt. Rev. Rowan Williams describes this critique succinctly in his observation that "any civilization must be capable of regularly asking itself questions about its purpose and integrity."[5]

Prophecy in the Jewish tradition is a forceful reminder that the state, the commonwealth, is always subject to sacred critique, because of being a partner in the divine purpose for life on earth. Although at present American society is a little vague on our partnership with God, I believe it behooves us to remember our founding in God's blessing and be faithful to those beginnings. Prophecy is a significant ingredient supplying sustained purpose and integrity.

This book will return again and again to these two foundations, Benedictine wisdom and the tradition of Old Testament prophecy. From these foundations, we will find strong resources first to support and sustain a *clarity of vision* concerning the reality of our distorted and diminished American public policy, and second, ways to gather personal and communal strength in order to *effectively challenge* the de-formations that are closing the doors to a more compassionate and life-giving public stance. These are the tasks now given to us: (1) clear and honest witness, and (2) a consistent and effective challenge to greed, harsh and war-filled governance, climate decay and danger, and structural racism.

Grounded in Benedictine and prophetic faith foundations, the first section of this book returns to the fact that, although the US was formed under the ideal of a benevolent God supporting our fledgling democracy, that ideal has been gradually de-formed by major cultural influences, and we Americans are largely in denial about the seriousness of our de-formation. In section II, the de-forming cultural influences that today are causing considerable suffering here and abroad are defined and described as (1) a pervasive market culture, (2) the expanding American empire, (3) the desperate decline in the health of our planet, and (4) an increasingly severe refusal of diversity.

Recovery from suffering begins with facing the truth of the displacement of God onto these four American idols. Such distortions of the sacred in our political life have caused a spiritual crisis in the US that cries out for healing. The third section of this book explicitly describes and recommends the strengths that Benedictine spirituality and prophetic imagination offer to energize and bring healing to our public life.

Here I share my concerns and reflections with you, the reader. May God bless our ongoing conversation in America.

Section I

America's Promise

CHAPTER ONE

America's Beginnings

I pray that the God of our Lord Jesus Christ, the Father
of glory, may give you a spirit of wisdom and revelation
as you come to know [God], so that, with the eyes of your
heart enlightened, you may know what is the hope to
which [you are] called. (Eph 1:17-18)

This book is a call for an active role for the sacred in American public policy. It is founded in the heritage of the Old Testament tradition of prophetic witness and in the pre- and post-Reformation tradition of Benedictine spirituality. Both of these can be faithful guides for many of us, Christian and others, as we gather the information and wisdom needed to challenge de-forming public policies. My understanding of an ongoing Christian life of faith is expressed in the term "spiritual formation." When our thoughts and actions are not congruent with that process, described in section III, the result is what I call "de-formation." Hence, section II next is devoted to the cultural expression of that de-formation widely expressed in our time. My thesis is that contemporary America has lost hope for the future and is numbed and discouraged by the absence of persistent, visible, and powerful advocacy for sacred values in our common life. And I propose in this book (1) to expose four principal policy choices that are de-forming contemporary American polity, and (2) to offer from my two primary foundations first, clear witness of the actual shape of current American public policies, and second, communal spiritual practices powerful enough to effectively challenge these choices that distort our avowed intentions as a nation.

As proposed here, the term "sacred" is not to be understood as the polar opposite to "secular," but rather as a vivid perception of everyday life as drenched in awe and wonder. To limit the sacred to fixed concepts of any religion is to make it too small. To see the sacred rightly in our current post-secular time requires a move "beyond the naïveté of first faith, with its childish certainties, facile assumptions, and acquired presuppositions or dogmas, into an open space of possibility,"[1] a possibility revealing the presence of something both utterly beyond human certainties and as persistently near us as our breath. Many religions not only have a concept of divinity at their center, but also affirm that the sacred spark is embodied in all that exists—people, plants, and animals, even the planet itself. The term "sacred" is also meant to suggest a quality of agency and presence, within and beyond time and space, something not within the control or even the full understanding of human beings. Modern religious language tends to differentiate between the term *pantheism*, which denotes the Divine as literally embodied in, say, a mountain or an animal, and a separate term, *panentheism*, which denies that the sacred is *confined* to a particular mountain or animal but affirms that the sacred is nevertheless visible in *all* that surrounds us, for those with eyes to see. It is this quality of the sacred that I urge must find expression in public policy, that is, the sense in which every person, every creature, every plant, even planet Earth bears something of the sacredness of life itself, a conception that also carries ethical demands for compassionate engagement with the sacred, wherever and whenever it appears.

For example, although the first biblical book of Genesis uses the term "dominion" to describe the responsibility given to humans for the world just created, dominion necessarily includes care and tending for every living thing that moves over the earth, because of God's evaluation that "indeed, it was very good" (Gen 1:28, 31). In the Christian New Testament,

Jesus affirms his sense of the sacred in every person with his closing instructions in Matthew's Gospel (25:35-40), "I was hungry and you gave me food, I was thirsty and you gave me something to drink . . . just as you did it to one of the least of these . . ., you did it to me." In much of Hinduism, while Brahman is the sole and ultimate reality, the soul within each being (the Atman) is linked with that Supreme Reality. Sufi Muslims conceive the contemplative human being as the *barzakh*, or isthmus, that connects God and the created world, transmitting to the created world the light and truth of God while also communicating the twinkling reflections of the created world back to God.[2] The sacredness shared among the One who is most holy and all creation itself is the basis for just and compassionate action on behalf of the poor and the marginalized. This basic concept forms a reality on which all religions can meet and journey together.[3]

As a cradle Christian myself, though for fifteen years committed to social justice with no specific claim of faith, I speak in this book with primary examples from my current perspective of Christian faith and scholarship, although I am very much aware that other religions and spiritualities contain similar examples and stories. Hence, the values that the sacred can and should specifically bring to our country are born in the spark of the Divine that resides in every living thing and must not be diminished or destroyed. The aim to include the sacred in our political life is intended to remind us of our human responsibility for the well-being of all. It calls forth justice for our local and global neighbors with whom our lives are inevitably linked. Also, the presence of the sacred in our political life reminds us that this is not a task for individuals alone but for communities of concerned people, and that our communal efforts must be attuned to the timing, the call, and the strength of the holy energies that surround us.

Another way to envision the significance of the sacred is to consider a major work of German theologian and philosopher Rudolph Otto in the early twentieth century titled, *The Idea of the Holy*.[4] Endeavoring to describe the mystery of the Holy, Otto first points out that the term "holy" (or sacred) contains a certain moral significance, but must be understood also as containing what he calls " a clear overplus of meaning."[5] After careful discussion of a variety of terms to be considered, Otto coins the Latin term, *mysterium tremendum et fascinans*, roughly translated as "tremendous and fascinating mystery." Even at a time of the growing influence of the scientific method, Otto persists in affirming an existence hidden at the core of all religious experience, distinct from rationality and morality. Otto saw the sacred as *numinous*, something "entirely other" that evokes the experience of a mysterious terror and awe and majesty, something incapable of being expressed directly in human language. While science with its empirical method is enormously helpful to us humans in many ways, today we are becoming aware that the comprehension of matters of the heart, art and music, and especially the holy requires tools beyond the reach of empiricism. I also urge that public policy deliberations are too important to be limited to technical expertise, empirical data, and economic considerations.

I am calling our people (you and me) to truthful self-examination, to (1) *witness* the actual intent and effect of our current American domestic and foreign policies, as well as to (2) community-initiated *challenge* to policies that are causing suffering and destruction to many human beings and to the created world. When we look honestly at what we *do* as a country, we must re-evaluate who we say we *are*. As twentieth-century Polish-born American rabbi and theologian Abraham Heschel urges, "the prophets remind us of the moral state of a people: Few are guilty, but all are responsible."[6]

I believe in the founding values of the United States of America, and I am proud to be a citizen of this country. In general, I think we are and intend to be a good people. And I also believe in God, and in God's generous and surprising intention for full freedom and joyous fulfillment for all the beings of the earth, an intention that is always beyond what we humans alone can and will create. I believe that when we are able to look honestly at America's contemporary role in the world, we must acknowledge and grieve that we have lost our way and harmed many. There is a better way forward; it is not too late. We still have time to take up the challenge of creating and sustaining a world that brings good news to the poor, release to the captives, and recovery of sight to the blind (Luke 4:18).

The content of this book is as follows: Section I: America's Promise, reviews the beginnings of the US as a democratic republic founded under the laws of nature and nature's God, and then considers two possible wake-up calls to the contemporary reality that our leaders and people deny and ignore. Section II, Witness to De-Formation: The Pathos of God, honestly witnesses what our country has become, in light of (1) our uncritical confidence in market culture, (2) overweening growth in our global empire, (3) denial of our earth's climate crisis, and (4) fear of and resistance to genuine diversity. These four dimensions of our dominant public policies demonstrate an arrogant disregard for "the beloved community," a term Dr. Martin Luther King Jr. brought to us, summarizing his hope for a strong and compassionate people under God. Section III, Formative Challenge to Public Policies, follows that stark witness to America's present condition, first urging us to realize our implicit consent to these realities and lamenting what we have lost. Lament leads next to conversion, linking spiritual practice with social change, and thereby bringing our people renewed hope and energy. Section III further offers imaginative prophetic strength for the communal work of ongoing challenge to de-formed public policy, founded in spiritual practices tried and true in 1,500 years of Benedictine life and the even longer heritage of Hebrew prophecy. The work will not be easy. Even reading about the facts laid out in section II may cause discomfort and grief to you, as it does to me. Yet I am persuaded that shared honesty, grief, prayer, and spiritually founded action is the only and proven way back to wholeness for all.

The Sacred and Public Policy: America's Promise

Although today we tend to regard the absolute separation of church and state as being enshrined in our founding documents, this is to misunderstand the possible role of the sacred in American life. Americans who are not familiar with the relationship of church and state in England (once our "mother country") or with the bloody history of England in the sixteenth and seventeenth centuries may not have a sense of what our early settlers were resisting in their insistence on such a separation. Even today in England, your street address defines you as a member of the local Anglican parish, which means you are entitled to be baptized, married, and buried in that place. (Today, you may choose not to do so, but you are nevertheless so entitled.) Avid seekers of family genealogies know that the most reliable early English information on births and deaths can be found not in the county civil office, but in the local parish register. Outside the authorized church, a person had no identity, no real existence. That intimate binding of person to the state-specified church is what the Puritans rejected. In addition, during a dreadful period of over one hundred years the English state authorities (kings and queens) directed brutal suppression (hangings, disembodiment, burning alive) of anyone who wished to worship at a place and in a manner different from that of the established church. The intimate union of church and state caused untold suffering in England, particularly when royal rules changed radically from decade to decade.

The US was founded during a period when European nations were making a momentous shift in understanding legitimate authority in governance of the state. In England, the establishment of a parliament to govern alongside the monarchy and the decision to separate national matters from the world church's theological and political control were undermining the power of both state and church. Similar events on the Continent increased the problem of authority. The great new political philosophies of the sixteenth and seventeenth centuries were proposing a view of humankind with remarkable independence of mind and an ability to manage worldly events. Political philosopher John Locke struggled to articulate the nature of an authority that no longer relied on powerful external institutions, rather resting entirely on an individual human's rational judgment. Natural rights philosophers were probing the question, "Under the circumstances of individual human freedom from control of church or state, what could persuade or constrain a person to limit such freedom, as the person becomes a member of society?" The answer, which seemed adequate at that time, was the establishment of a theoretical "social contract." The social contract provided a means for men to transfer conditionally some of their individual rights to a government whose primary duty was to ensure stable and comfortable enjoyment of those natural rights. Individuals retained their basic rights from a government employed to act on their behalf and also maintained the power to restrain that government (by popular vote), should it exceed or manipulate its powers against those natural freedoms.[7]

In making the case that men were free and equal by nature and could safely rely on their own reasoning mind, the natural rights philosophy also made the case that individuals were no longer under serious obligation to any monarch or church authority. At the time, little attention was paid to the means necessary to build such mature, reasoning, compassionate minds (as it was assumed that everyone who mattered had them). A nod was made to the notion that individuals bore a certain reciprocal responsibility to obey laws adopted under the social contract. But the emphasis both in natural rights philosophy and in democratic theory was placed on the freedom of individuals to exercise their rights without interference. Briefly, it is of value to note that in those centuries, the word "men" actually meant "White, propertied men." Subsequent centuries and amendments to our Constitution have expanded this field to include a much-broadened group of people, including women, people of color, and indigenous people. But the limitations of this early definition have heavily contributed to subsequent problems, given that the construction of the mature, reasoning mind was unthinkingly attributed to the specialized education accorded to White men of property, while excluding many intuitive understandings of a broader, natural, and "beyond-rational" world. To ensure this limited meaning, our founders added a republican (representative, rather than egalitarian) dimension to our founding documents.

While these philosophical matters were being debated in Europe and the US, our new American republic was beginning to take shape. The American founders rejected church control of the state as well as state control of the church, but still considered the benevolence of God to be an important ingredient in our emerging polity. They called upon an orderly God (not one linked to any particular religion or church), to justify their rational decision to separate legally from England and to frame the basic documents molding the new nation. While creating a new political entity, our founders felt it necessary to weave the concept of an overarching deity and his (sic) purposes into their reflections and documents. The concept of theistic religion gave sacred legitimacy to the new democratic order. As examples, consider what Jefferson and Washington said about the role of religion in our republic.

Thomas Jefferson, in the Declaration of Independence, refers four times to God. The first sentence speaks of the "laws of Nature and Nature's God" that entitle any people to be independent. The second is the lynchpin of the Declaration, that "all men are endowed by their Creator with certain inalienable Rights." The last two occurrences, referring to natural law and biblical religion, locate the legitimacy of the new nation in a conception of "higher law," appealing to "the Supreme Judge of the world for the rectitude of our intentions," firmly relying on "the protection of divine Providence." George Washington affirms that "Of all the dispositions and habits which lead to political prosperity, Religion and Morality are indispensable supports." Even the sometimes-irreverent Benjamin Franklin observes, "I never was without some religious principles. I never doubted, for instance, the existence of the Deity; that he made the world and governed it by his Providence, that the most acceptable service of God was the doing of good to men; that our souls are immortal; and that all crime will be punished and virtue rewarded, either here or hereafter."[8]

The conviction that God supported the establishment of our new nation was intimately linked to our founders' belief that America bore a special divine destiny, not unlike that of the ancestral Hebrews' sense of being a chosen people.[9] The ideas that infused the nation and the people drawn to settle here were seen to represent the highest and best in human values and the corresponding responsibility to extend and share those values with other peoples and countries. The sense of a special destiny continues to this day as a significant part of the American sense of self-understanding, even in the face of a growing secularism in the culture, as a whole. The circumstances of our founding and continued success as a democratic experiment, in the face of the tragic unfolding of the French attempt at democracy and the continuing preference of the European nations for monarchy, created confidence in the special virtues of our American people and institutions.

Such a destiny under God is made clear in the Puritan John Winthrop's sermon envisioning the virtuous American community as a "city on a hill," a shining example to the Old World (Europe). The Louisiana Purchase and America's various territorial expansions to the Pacific coast seemed to confirm this ambition, and the phrase "manifest destiny" began to fall from many lips. President Lincoln's Gettysburg Address followed later, asking and hoping that a nation conceived with our democratic and godly ideals would long survive. Memorial Day, a national holiday growing out of the Civil War, gave ritual expression to American destiny, including "a rededication to the martyred dead, to the spirit of sacrifice, and to the

American vision."[10] Even John F. Kennedy's inaugural address in 1961 carries forward these themes of divine blessing. He notes that although his world was very different from that of the founders, "the same revolutionary beliefs for which our forebears fought are still at issue . . . the belief that the rights of man come not from the generosity of the state but from the hand of God." While affirming that sovereignty rests with the people, Kennedy also acknowledged that basic human rights are rooted in a source higher than any political structure.[11]

These paragraphs are intended to clarify why, despite a clear separation of the boundaries of church and state, America has been, since its beginnings, dependent on at least an implicit relationship of religion and politics. To be sure, tension has always existed in America between church and state, but increasingly it is clear that religion is not going away, even as our culture becomes more rational and scientific. Today we are in what has been described as a "post-secular period," not so much because of a sudden increase in religiosity, but rather a sense that something of the Spirit of God remains vital.

America's religious ideas and ideals, wrapped in our founding, still sustain us as our collective narrative or "myth." The language used above is very familiar, and though derived from Protestant Christianity, it is not itself Christian. However, although the deity invoked is somewhat austere, he is also actively interested and involved in history, especially America's history. The foundational concepts of America closely resemble the covenant Yahweh made with ancient Israel, promising to bring them to a land of milk and honey where they would establish a new social order. Note that, in both cases, the promised land was already occupied, but it was understood that God promised to make Israel and America victorious against those they must defeat in order to obtain possession, so long as the people remained in covenant with God. In general, the role prescribed for the American democratic deity is to be useful, oriented to what this deity will do for us. An active and interested citizenry is expected, but no method is specifically established to create and sustain such citizens.

The ideals of this narrative of America as God's chosen people persist in deeply embedded cultural codes that still provide a blueprint not only for institutions, but also for social and psychological processes. Our sustained ideals contribute to a highly positive self-image, seldom burdened with examination or critique. Because we as a people seldom review our country's actual history or current behavior, increasingly we are out of touch with the distressing impact of our political policies at home and abroad. Chapter 2 next recounts two recent, potential "wake-up calls" to America, as well as why we have mostly ignored or denied what they could tell us. We cannot forever avoid laying bare the shadow side of our history; even our founding values can be good guides to that reassessment, if broadened in practice to include many who now suffer and are left out. Also, America has a long tradition of painful critiques of the ways we have fallen short, and attending to those may help us be restored to the kind of people our founders claimed for us.[12]

Political Theology

A relatively new term has appeared in the last decade suggesting an ongoing interaction of politics and religion. The term, "political theology," describes a reality rooted in human history. Initially this term may seem a paradox to us, but political theology is the long-practiced study of the ever-changing relationships between political community and religious wisdom.[13] Taken as a whole, religious traditions of the world contain significant wisdom about how to respond to the struggles that humans are likely to experience, about the most generous ways to engage with one another for the best of all concerned, and about practices that best develop inner peace and outward justice. Though wisdom begins with notions of righteousness and compassion, it goes beyond that. Political theology suggests a close linkage between the political and the spiritual in terms of community bonding and shared decision-making, while not asserting the superiority of either politics or religion in general. The term "sacred," when used in reference to the "theology" part of political theology, offers effective ways to invite and respond to the divine presence within history and politics, whether or not so perceived.

Political theology informs the chapters of this book, as a way of making visible and embodying sacred values in our *shared common good*. In general, political theology becomes an issue in times of crisis, when the relationships between politics and religion are changing, as they were, for example, during the seventeenth-century Enlightenment, when the concept of democratic government emerged, free from control of church or monarch. I propose that a similar crisis has emerged in the contemporary post-secular period, which is not unlike those long-ago days when Plato and Aristotle struggled with fundamental questions of human life in community. In that early Greek period of Western philosophy, our present rigid distinction between political theory and theology did not exist. Instead, the principal concerns of both dealt with foundational human issues: then as now, the questions pertained to the most fruitful ways to live with one another, given differing human temperaments and conflicting values. The Greek city-state, called the *polis*, was seen as the arena that shaped human personality (and vice versa) to fulfill human potential and to work together effectively. As we know, Greek city-states did not live up to their ideal, but the ideal itself lasted for centuries, notably somewhat like the ideal of community in Judeo-Christian life.

Reflecting on political theology today, American philosopher, political activist, and social critic Cornel West makes a distinction between what he calls "Constantinian Christianity," and "prophetic Christianity."[14] Constantinian Christianity came into being in 313 CE, when the Roman Emperor Constantine declared Christianity to be the official religion of his empire, causing Christianity gradually to draw away from its seminal values as it was absorbed into Rome's imperialist aims. West suggests a similar shift has taken place in some contemporary American Christian communities, where nationalist values in the emerging American empire have been absorbed into the Christian view, thus re-forming or de-forming previous values articulated in the New Testament.

Old Testament theologian Walter Brueggemann identifies a similar absorption of other peoples by what he calls "royal consciousness."[15] Both in Egypt at the time of Moses and in Rome at the time of Constantine, a fundamental orientation toward the sacred was diluted until diminished in favor of the dominant royal power. Constantinian Christianity today emphasizes personal conversion, individual piety, and philanthropic service, while prophetic Christianity focuses on living with humility, loving our neighbors, and doing unto others as we would have them do unto us.[16] The perspective in this book about the nature of the sacred is closely linked to prophetic Judaism and Christian spirituality. As such, the central question for us is, how do we restore a society rooted in what might be called "godly values," rather than national or indeed imperial goals that have de-formed us as individuals and broken our community spirit?

Founding Heritages

The two major foundations that inform this book are Old Testament prophecy and Benedictine spirituality, both of which lend themselves to an amalgam of the old and the new.[17] Both offer "new wine" that will inevitably burst old wineskins even as they are faithful to the Yahweh and Jesus of Scripture. The new wine is blended by wise stewards who can be openhearted in the face of necessary losses yet faithfully imaginative about "possible worlds." "Possible worlds" is twentieth-century philosopher Paul Ricoeur's term for the astonishing surprise of encountering previously unimaginable realities.[18] Twelfth-century Jewish philosopher Maimonides also anticipates the idea of possible worlds in his statement that "the prophetic hope is belief in the 'plausibility of the possible,' as opposed to the 'necessity of the probable.'"[19]

The Tradition of Prophecy

Cornel West speaks of "prophetic Christianity" and Walter Brueggemann's classic book is called *The Prophetic Imagination*. What, then, is prophecy? Today it is sometimes thought that prophecy involves prediction of the future, but tradition does not understand prophecy that way. Brueggemann insists that "alternative futures are not derived from, or determined by, the present."[20] The vision of the prophet is twofold: on the one hand, the prophet must have a keen perception of what is happening in his or her society at present; and on the other hand, the prophet is listening attentively to and for the word of God. In short, the prophet's eye is on the contemporary scene and her ear is inclined to God.[21] However, the prophet's understanding of the present moment is focused less on any immediate crisis and more on a God-informed vision of a cultural crisis that is enduring and resilient, but which may still be somewhat invisible to the community at large. In other words, the "issue" that is the focus of God's concern (and the prophet's) is fundamentally that of a widespread but deforming cultural consciousness.

Brueggemann distinguishes between two types of cultural consciousness, one being a "totalism," which he initially called "royal consciousness," with reference to Pharoah's Egypt and the Davidic kingship line after David's death. Throughout this book, I will call that type "imperial consciousness," which I think is congruent with Brueggemann's understanding and updated to the present time and place. This totalism type of cultural consciousness is a carefully managed approach by those currently in power; and *its purpose is solely to secure and defend its own power*. Totalism cannot tolerate criticism and will go to great lengths to suppress, co-opt, or otherwise defeat any serious challenge to its worldview. Imperial consciousness prospers by causing people to believe that *no other way of functioning is thinkable* or can even be tried. Totalism also uses phony moral claims to stay in control, and/or to deny that any genuine suffering or hurt exists within the imperial realm.

Brueggemann's second form of cultural consciousness is open-ended, allowing and even encouraging imaginative alternative visions for a new social reality, in particular, the genuine possibilities for justice and compassion among the people. The work of the prophet is first to uncover places where the community has failed to live up to its side of a covenant, its sacred aspirations. The prophet discerns where public policy has allowed (if not caused) inequities to flourish, and to make those failures and inequities visible to all. It is the prophet's task to speak the sacred truth, to make the concern and care of the invisible God now visible, and hopefully, to energize and empower action in and by the people. The reason why the prophet can never say, "this is the way it will be," is because the unfolding future always depends on whether and how the people respond to the prophetic word.

Once the prophet experiences the inspiration of God, the next step is to find a powerful way and a central place to convey God's concern and dismay about the shape and effects of the imperial consciousness. Contemporary scholars of prophecy insist that the word of God's judgment is also a word of God's suffering with the hurts of humanity. Apart from advocacy for social change, the prophet's speech has the primary purpose of clearly revealing "the extreme pertinence of humans to God, God's world-directedness, attentiveness and concern."[22] The term Heschel uses to describe God's presence and engagement in human history is "pathos." He elaborates:

> The predicament of humans is a predicament of God Who has a stake in the human situation. . . . The divine pathos, the fact of God's participation in the predicament of humans, is the elemental fact. The essential meaning of pathos is, therefore, not to be seen in its psychological denotation, as standing for a state of the (human) soul, but in its theological connotation, signifying God as involved in history.[23]

Yet, even as pathos is an essential moment in prophecy, so is the ability "to pivot, to talk with confidence that God is working out an alternative world of well-being, of justice, of peace, of security—in spite of the contradictions . . . Suffering is also healing, for the promise of the gospel is that the powers and principalities will yield to human agency that is authorized and powered by God . . . We hear this promise not only in good preaching but also in rap music and other hopeful and dynamic places."[24]

Being a prophet is not easy, for the prophet not only receives God's word, participates in the pathos/suffering of God, and sings with joy and hope in God's promises. The prophet experiences God's pain, in all its vulnerability, grief, anger, joy, and passion. Suffering is central to prophetic consciousness, in part as a sharing in the pathos of God and in part because when the prophet is effective, he or she necessarily will also intensify the people's suffering.[25] Suffering is the signal that the people have heard and are responding to God's prophetic call. Given the overall numbness characteristic of a community kept under the control of an imperial consciousness, the experience of lament and pathos is a relief because it is experienced as a first step away from numbness and toward return and renewal.

The first evidence of communal response to the prophet is grief for what has been lost, because the release of grief is a necessary step toward the renewal brought by an alternative consciousness. Following the release of grief comes confidence in renewal, and energy to reject the present imperialist ordering of things, making the decision to change, and embracing the promise of another realistic possibility toward which the community may move.[26] This book will show how prophetic imagination and Benedictine spirituality can provide and sustain such confidence.

Is prophecy relevant to our age and place? Given the general secularity (or post-secularity) of our times, it may seem that prophecy is irrelevant. As a broad community, we may or may not be willing to acknowledge the reality of a God-like presence in human history. Perhaps the problem is that it is difficult to summon up an image of God different from the stock old fellow with a beard sitting on a throne in heaven. On the other hand, many of us tell pollsters that we believe in God, and even talk with God regularly. I suspect that many have also had moments of what we might call inspiration that surprised us and seemed to come from nowhere. I hope that you might be able to suspend any disbelief long enough to hear (and share?) what seems to be the voice of prophecy for our time, a critical and loving assessment of the issues laid out in section II of this book. If that makes sense to you, perhaps you will join me (and God) in grief for the dominance of present-day imperial consciousness and passion for what might prophetically come into existence. I hope too that you will find resources here that restore you to hope for an alternative future in which we can learn to think and act as our best and most loving selves. With that prayer, we turn to consider our second foundation in Benedictine spirituality.

The Relevance of Benedictine Spirituality

As a Benedictine oblate, I understand Benedict to be always asking the question, "What does it mean to live as God would have us live, *in times like these*?" The man we now call St. Benedict was born in the last decades of the fifth century, in a small town north of Rome, approximately seventy years after the (so-called) barbarian Alaric conquered Rome, ending the grand ambition of the Pax Romana. Benedict's times suffered an inflationary economy, small wandering bands of recently unemployed soldiers, intense poverty, extortionate taxes, and the beginning of what are now called "the Dark Ages." After a solid boyhood education and several years as a hermit praying and meditating on Scripture, Benedictine returned to society and eventually founded a monastery at Monte Cassino in Italy. Drawing on manuscripts available to him, Benedict (with the help of his twin sister, I'd like to think) wrote an outline for monastic practice in community, called the *Regula*, or Rule. It

was such an openhearted, sound, and realistic document that
monastics today still live under the guidance of that Rule. In
the last thirty years or so, an increasing number of lay people
who live the common life (called oblates) have taken up the
Rule as an aid to faithfully living the Gospel. While written
for monastics who would live in cloistered community, Benedict's Rule also demonstrates that valuable opportunities for
spiritual (as well as psychological and social) renewal lie precisely in noticing and amending our faults, revealed in interaction with others and the community. The truth of this insight
is such that more and more "ordinary people" worldwide have
chosen to become Benedictine "oblates," receiving guidance
from monastics for a spiritual life focused on seeking God
within the ordinary moments of the day, of continuing to take
up dialogue between the apparently secular world and the
assurance of the divine presence with us always.[27]

Later in this book, we'll look at the specific elements Benedict recommends as a means to develop personal and communal spiritual maturity, and effective participation in public
life. Now we look at how the way of life Benedict describes in
his Rule can be helpful in bringing the sacred into public life.
An invaluable resource for that purpose is a speech made by
then-archbishop of the Anglican Communion, the Rt. Rev.
Rowan Williams, where he describes Benedict and his Rule as
offering a model for civic virtue.[28] Fr. Williams was probing
how we humans can sustain a civilization capable of asking
itself questions about its purpose and its integrity. Noting that
the Rule did not set out to save civilization (though it emerged
at the cusp of the so-called Dark Ages, and monasteries often
have been honored during this difficult period as guardians
of the books of civilization, safe places for travelers to stay
overnight, providers of food for the hungry, and always generous hospitality), Williams observes that the *Rule defines in itself
the components* of a certain kind of civilization. While it is sometimes thought that Benedict prescribed a withdrawal into enclaves where the memory of civilization was preserved but

not understood, that is to misunderstand the Rule. Instead, Williams proposes that Benedict's guidelines for life in a monastery make a positive contribution toward modeling the active Christian life, offering a sketch of political or civic virtue rooted in Christianity. Quotations in the paragraphs below are extracted from that speech.

Williams asks, "If there is a civilization to be saved, what are the dimensions of the Rule that point us towards the essentials that have to be preserved and nourished?" To put it another way, what are the political virtues that the Rule generates? Williams responds with three particular aspects of the Rule: time, obedience, and participation.

Time. Williams is not so much concerned with Benedict's specified daily schedule as with the question we must all ask of our lives: Given how we spend our time (generally today either working or consuming), what sort of self are we building? We must be productive, but are we just a cog in a production machine? Is our labor something congenial to our personal conditions and capacities? Are our minds and hearts self-aware and also Other/other-aware? If not, can we set aside time for the study and reflection that build awareness of joy and satisfaction in service? Can we be at peace in quiet moments? Before reading on, take a few moments now to ask these questions of yourself and of your various communities.

Williams concludes that the civic contribution made by the appropriate use of time is the continuous awareness, as we establish and support public policy, that the culture we are creating is the context in which humanity is allowed (or not) to grow—in memory, intelligence, and love. These matters call for personal consideration, not only in our own lives, but also as we build and participate in family, community, and nation. What kind of context does our use of time create for our ongoing personal and communal formation? Surely it cannot be good for us to rush from one project to another. Surely it cannot be good for human beings to be pressured to produce more and more in less and less time.

Obedience. Many of us are not comfortable with the word obedience, thinking it means domination by an individual will. But obedience in the Rule is highly nuanced; the abbot, who is the leader, is him- or herself required to be obedient both to the Rule governing everyone and to a sensitive awareness of each member of the community. Benedictine obedience, according to Williams, is intended to create the "immense, elusive goal of a common life in which each can recognize their good and their flourishing in the life they share." The root form of the word "obedience" refers to a deep listening that is both interior and exterior, to oneself, to other persons, to the overall energy of the community, and to God. The Rule is specific that each member should strive to outdo each other *in only one regard*, and that is mutual respect (RB 72.4). While attentive listening to the whole community is primarily the superior's responsibility, every member of the community is also called to that task. Benedict even suggests that sometimes the most youthful member may be sensitive to something the rest have not noticed (RB 3.3).

The civic contribution made by the practice of obedience is that each person's standing is defined, not by any external criterion such as wealth or social status or education or even chronological age, but solely by the scope of one's involvement in community life. Furthermore, the less materially advantaged members should be allowed and encouraged to offer their unique voice in the shaping of the common life. Overall balances need to be adjusted periodically to "incorporate both the gifts and needs of the incoming stranger . . . who is seeking shared belonging." Later in this book we will consider the way animal and plant communities are strengthened by biodiversity. Much the same may be true of human communities as we consider the impact and value of immigrants and refugees seeking shared belonging. Obedience, shared deep listening, and welcome to one another offer considerable blessings, as Abraham and Sarah discovered in welcoming strangers at Mamre (Gen 18).

Participation. Participation is the third key theme of the Rule emphasized by Williams. Each member of the community is to be "active in the common work of the community, even if they are unwell or not particularly competent." The Rule of Benedict requires that each person takes a positive and distinctive share in sustaining the communal life, and also gives to each the dignity of responsibility for that life in order to create what Williams calls an "intelligent corporate ecology." The civic benefit created by full participation is that it sets free the specific contribution of each member, without which the community would be incomplete or unhealthy.

We'll return to this theme again at the beginning of chapter 6, on biodiversity. The evidence is clear in plant and animal communities that the whole is healthier with the contributions of many diverse individuals. Participation is "partly about the diffusion of economic resources," but it also requires "the preservation of minority culture and language." Williams observes that public policy in a moral world society must take seriously the ethical question of "how to avoid creating perpetually dependent and powerless enclaves" that have no scope for full economic freedom in the global market. This aspect of the Rule in particular challenges the contemporary reality of global empire discussed below in section II. The Rule of Benedict expresses a "clear and unambiguous assumption that there is such a thing as a common good," and therefore undergirds a principle of public policy that all things should work together for that good. And, Williams concludes, in light of a fundamental concern for the sacred to be expressed in public policy, it should be clear that "the whole ethos and direction of the common life has to return continually to the praise of God, the most central and significant aspect of this life together."

CHAPTER TWO

Called to Account

The Lord sent a word against Jacob,
and it fell on Israel;
and all the people knew it . . .
but in pride and arrogance of heart they said:
"The bricks have fallen,
but we will build with dressed stones;
the sycamores have been cut down,
but we will put cedars in their place."
So the LORD raised adversaries against them,
and stirred up their enemies. . . .
For all this his anger has not turned away,
his hand is stretched out still. (Isa 9:8-12)

A Benevolent World Presence?

After the fall of the Berlin Wall in 1989, and the final dissolution of the Soviet Union in 1991 due to internal revolutions, the United States was the lone remaining superpower in the world. Americans continued to cherish the idea that our democratic experiment was divinely ordained and that God's hand was expressed in our polity, and that our "willingness" to extend the benefits of democracy was a gift to the world. Nonetheless, the dissenting religious tradition of our Puritan settlers remained strong, so that neither government in general nor government interference in religion were to be trusted. As a result, American citizens tended to prefer that government be as limited as possible.[1] This "dissenting" viewpoint also meant that American citizens tended to be isolationists, preferring small, local government and limited international engagement, even as we felt some obligation to share our democratic blessings with other countries.

Dissenting churches "tend to see society and the world as split between the righteous and the unrighteous."[2] This heritage means that we generally are conflicted about foreign policy, and that when we do engage with other nations, we are apt to do so as "saviors," eager to transform others into the "saved."[3] This perspective has meant that, rather than look squarely at the facts of our growing dominance in world affairs, we prefer to rest in noble platitudes, such as that our country did not seek but rather "had greatness thrust upon us."[4]

During the late twentieth century, some politicians spoke approvingly about the possibility that the US was becoming an empire, but as the reality became more vivid, the term was minimized as contrary to our people's self-image. During the years of superpower standoff with the Soviet Union, American containment of the "evil empire" had seemed to require the development of "hundreds of installations around the world for the largest military we ever maintained in peacetime," thus making it seem that this widespread military presence was not a form of imperialism.[5] When the Soviet Union fragmented, the US was faced with the need and the opportunity to reconsider its international role. If, in fact, America's stated foreign policy objectives were limited—"to protect our homeland, to preserve our values, to defend our closest allies"—the collapse of the Soviet Union presented the opportunity to greatly reduce the military budget and overseas deployments.[6] But that did not happen; by then, the temptations of worldwide power were too great. Instead, the US began to use military power to advance its commercial interests.[7] America employed its vast military presence, in the language of conservative commentator Andrew Bacevich, "not merely in response to a crisis, but to anticipate, intimidate, preempt, and control. And it did so routinely and continuously."[8]

A Military Attack on Our Homeland and Our Response

On the morning of September 11, 2001, America woke to the unthinkable: an attack on the soil of the United States. Possibly our citizens had not thought of New York City's World Trade Center or the Pentagon in Washington, DC, as the symbolic headquarters of a world empire, but clearly members of the radical Islamic group al-Qaeda did. After hijacking four American civilian airplanes, the terrorists carried out a highly orchestrated series of attacks, first by flying two airplanes into the north and south towers of the World Trade Center (which subsequently imploded), and next by flying another plane into the Pentagon. The fourth plane crashed in rural Pennsylvania when a heroic passenger rebellion thwarted that mission, which presumably had been directed at the White House. In all, 3,000 people were killed. The attacks were seen on television by Americans in every state, creating a memorable and terrifying crisis across the country.

For the first few days afterwards, the focus seemed to be on the bravery of the firemen and relief organizations who rushed to assist, some dying in the continuing fires. People flocked to blood banks and donated money to help. The American mood was of general goodwill, heightened civility, and generous kindness throughout the country. "There was a substantive discussion about what it is about the nature of the American presence in the world that created a situation in which movements like al-Qaeda can thrive and prosper."[9] But before a month had passed, this mood changed into a lust for revenge, including scattered violence against Muslims living in the US.[10] Some television shows began a campaign *against* those seeking to understand those who had attacked us. The theme of that campaign was that pure evil is beyond human understanding and can only be opposed, and that "any attempt to show that the US might bear some responsibility for conditions leading up to the attacks was . . . moral relativism."[11]

Declaring his responsibility to history to rid the world of evil, President George W. Bush and his cabinet responded in three major ways. First, a new cabinet-level Department of Homeland Security was created, responsible for preventing terrorist attacks, border security, immigrations and customs, and disaster relief and prevention. In the urgency of creating greater security for Americans, this new Department not only adopted punitive policies at our border with Mexico, but seriously limited American civil liberties.[12] Second, Bush ordered unilateral attacks on Iraq (though it had not been proven that Iraq had anything to do with the attacks on the USA) at the beginning of a declared "War on Terror." And third, the administration announced and adopted *The National Security Strategy of the United States of America* (NSS 2002), a document that introduced the doctrine of *preventive warfare*, allowing America to attack other countries *before* they pose an immediate threat.[13] This document declared, "America will strike any nation or any group that it deems dangerous, whenever and however it feels necessary, and regardless of provocation or lack thereof, . . . reserving the right to act with or without allies. No nation will be allowed to surpass or even equal American military power."[14]

Take a moment to read those words of the declaration again to understand the incredible step that America here takes in relation to all the other countries of the world! Consider NSS 2002 again, keeping in mind that it formally adopts many recommendations of a much earlier document called *Rebuilding America's Defenses*, published in 2000 by the neoconservative think tank, Project for the New American Century.[15] *Rebuilding America's Defenses* was first drafted in 1992 by the members of the Bush administration as a Defense Planning Guidance document, suggesting policies the US should consider, including greatly increased funding for military affairs, administered by a new branch of the military called the US Space Command, which was to "dominat[e] the space dimension of military operations to protect US national interests and investment."

This document concludes that "The emerging synergy of space superiority with land, sea, and air superiority, will lead to Full Spectrum Dominance."[16] The "space dimension of military operations" includes surveillance technology that can precisely identify enemies of the US on any part of the planet as well as a plan to weaponize space.[17]

The fact that ten years elapsed between the creation of this plan and its actual adoption suggests at least the possibility that the government had waited until American public opinion could be persuaded of its necessity by a shocking foreign assault. Nonetheless, full details of the plan set forth in *Rebuilding America's Defenses* were known by only a few people until May 2005, when a *New York Times* reporter quoted the head of the Space Command as defining his goal as "freedom to attack as well as freedom from attack."[18]

America did not fare well internationally in the aftermath of its violent responses to the 9/11 attacks. True, al-Qaeda partisans initiated the violence, but many people at home and abroad felt the USA overreacted and overreached. David Cole, professor at Georgetown University Law Center, reports on the federal government's disregard of basic human rights of foreign nationals, with about 5,000 Arab American and Muslim men being secretly detained under the antiterrorism initiative, as well as 650 enemy combatants locked up at Guantanamo Bay, being held without trial, without charges, without access to family or counsel.[19] The most serious international charge was that the US had undermined the rule of international law by attacking Iraq "preventatively" and "unilaterally," without the support of the United Nations nor with firm evidence that Iraq had harbored terrorists. The American government's reactions to the 9/11 attacks, especially the invasion of the personal privacy of Americans by the Department of Homeland Security using means such as wiretaps and searches, might in other times have been viewed as unconstitutional. Although a number of books by American authors expressing concern were published shortly afterwards, in general, the American public went along meekly. It is not a secret that nothing manufactures consent better than fear (in this case, of terrorists). In horror at an attack on our own land, and in response to governmentally induced hysteria, our appetite for revenge caused us to trade our freedoms for an illusion of security.[20]

The world was dismayed by the US attack on Iraq, and the declaration of the "war on terror." It was not long after that antiwar demonstrations took place in London and Paris, Belgium and Spain, in many other nations and in front of the United Nations building. Poet Judyth Hill responded with a poem, "Wage Peace," from which I quote the following lines:

> Wage peace with your breath.
>
> Breathe in firemen and rubble,
> breathe out whole buildings and flocks of red wing blackbirds.
>
> Breathe in terrorists
> and breathe out sleeping children and freshly mown
>   fields. . . .
>
> Make soup.
>
> Play music, memorize the words for thank you in three
>   languages. . . .
>
> Think of chaos as dancing raspberries,
> imagine grief
> as the outbreath of beauty
> or the gesture of fish
>
> Swim for the other side.
>
> Wage peace.[21]

Benedictine author and speaker Sister Joan Chittister also wrote a commentary on 9/11, including these words:

> What specific concerns drove these men to the point where they would give up their own lives just to injure ours is hard to tell. Few asked, and fewer still seemed to care. In the midst

of national grief—and for many, anger—all that mattered, apparently, was who to strike in retaliation. Anybody would do, it seemed. And so we did.

[The world changed] on the day when, without clear proof of Iraq's involvement, without undeniable certainty, without the approval of most of the world, the United States roared over Iraq on bombing raids. . . .

On that day—not long after the whole world had grieved with us over the merciless loss of 3,000 innocent US lives—the world divided in its loyalties, most of them against us.[22]

The most compelling of the 9/11 critiques I heard came from farmer, author, and poet Wendell Berry, called "Thoughts in the Presence of Fear." Because of its power, I am tempted to include the whole reflection, but in the interests of space will content myself by referring you to a website, and simply quote here a few of the introductory points.[23]

I. THE TIME WILL SOON COME when we will not be able to remember the horrors of September 11 without remembering also the unquestioning technological and economic optimism that ended on that day.

II. This optimism rested on the proposition that we were living in a "new world order" and a "new economy" that would "grow" on and on, bringing a prosperity of which every new increment would be "unprecedented."

III. The dominant politicians, corporate officers, and investors who believed this proposition did not acknowledge that the prosperity was limited to a tiny percent of the world's people, and to an ever smaller number of people even in the United States; that it was founded upon the oppressive labor of poor people all over the world; and that its ecological costs increasingly threatened all life, including the lives of the supposedly prosperous.

IV. The "developed" nations had given to the "free market" the status of a god, and were sacrificing to it their farmers, farmlands, and communities, their forests, wetlands, and prairies, their ecosystems and watersheds. They had accepted universal pollution and global warming as normal costs of doing business.

V. There was, as a consequence, a growing worldwide effort on behalf of economic decentralization, economic justice, and ecological responsibility. We must recognize that the events of September 11 make this effort more necessary than ever. We citizens of the industrial countries must continue the labor of self-criticism and self-correction. We must recognize our mistakes.

Post-9/11, America was a fearful country. We had never previously been invaded by an enemy, nor one without the status of a nation. We had thought ourselves secure, and we imagined ourselves unhated. The question that recurred again and again was, "Why do they hate us so much?"

I propose that the answer to this question lies in the fact that America had succumbed to an "imperialist consciousness," meaning that our leaders were undertaking actions to benefit a plutocratic elite in this country, while we citizens in general were in a benumbed state of ignorance and discouragement. The gift of 9/11 was that it was a wake-up call, an urgent invitation to become more self- and other-aware. We were called to a serious self-critique, and a small window existed when we might have answered that call. But we quickly moved instead into a position of military reaction and humanitarian denial. We refused the sacred opportunity.

The next portion of this chapter looks at another, more recent, wake-up call, the coronavirus pandemic of 2020. After exploring its dynamics, the chapter will continue with reflection on why denial has been a preferred strategy for our country in the face of such wake-up calls. The second section of this book undertakes the self-examination to which I believe these crises still call us today.

A Viral Attack on Our Homeland and Our Response

On December 31, 2019, China reported a cluster of cases of "pneumonia" in people associated with the Hunan Seafood Wholesale Market in Wuhan, Hubei Province. In January, Chinese health authorities confirmed that this cluster was associated with a novel coronavirus. Epidemiologic data subsequently indicated that person-to-person transmission of the disease was occurring outside the market area.[24] On January 30, 2020, the director-general of the World Health Organization, confirming the spread of the disease—now called COVID-19—to 18 countries outside China with 98 cases, as well as over 7,000 cases within China (including 170 deaths there), declared a public health emergency of international concern. By then, the first case had also appeared in the US. In his speech to the IHR Emergency Committee, WHO's director-general praised China for the speed with which they had "detected the outbreak, isolated the virus, sequenced the genome and shared it with WHO." Nevertheless, given the rapid spread to other countries, he confirmed that the virus was strong and deadly, and that it was essential for all countries "to work together in a spirit of solidarity and cooperation" to defeat the pandemic.[25]

The full energy of the scientific and public health communities worldwide was quickly directed to understanding the virus, exploring how it was transmitted, and what safety measures would best slow its spread. The search for a vaccine was initiated in several research centers, and it did not take long for a few key safety measures to be widely understood: wash hands frequently, wear masks, stay six feet apart from other people, shelter in place as much as possible. COVID-19 was primarily though not exclusively a respiratory disease, transmitted by droplets propelled from the mouth when speaking, and especially when shouting or singing. One confounding fact about COVID-19 was that it could be transmitted by asymptomatic carriers.

Since this book is being written during the COVID-19 pandemic, we do not yet know the full effects of the outbreak, nor do we have the benefit of hindsight (as we do with the 9/11 attacks). COVID-19 was creating chaos everywhere, and within several months, worldwide cases had topped twenty million, but our focus in this book is on the American experience. What was the situation with the disease in America several months into the pandemic? It is notable that, by faithfully following recommended guidelines, some other countries rigorously drove infection rates nearly to zero, while "coronavirus transmission in the United States was out of control. . . . The national US response was fragmented, shot through with political rancor and culture-war divisiveness."[26] With only 4 percent of the world's population, the US had 25 percent of known infections. How did this happen?

It was soon discovered that in the US, public health centers and supplies had been systematically declining for years. Local public health agencies, which depended largely on federal funding from the Centers for Disease Control and Prevention, had had their budgets cut by 30 percent since 2003.[27] Urgent needs for dealing with the pandemic were inadequate: items such as masks, personal protective equipment, and ventilators were in such scarce supply that individual states began competing with one another to purchase limited resources whose prices kept going up. The federal government declined to provide recommendations, initially denying that the virus was a problem and later assigning all responsibility for crisis management to the states.

As state health agencies across America began to process growing numbers of people who succumbed to the virus and as rules were put in place for people to self-quarantine or shelter-in-place, the virus began to take a toll on other aspects of American life, notably the economy. Employees were laid off or furloughed, those who could worked at home, schools were closed and children were told to do lessons virtually if broadband internet was available, and businesses went broke or filed for bankruptcy. In late March, the stock market dropped steeply, and the International Monetary Fund traced significant shrinkage in the global economy, forecasting an overall drop of 3 percent to the worldwide GDP, and estimating production losses of between 5 and 15 percent in the US alone.[28] In our country, where shopping and entertainment represent major parts of the economy yet were hardest hit by closures, citizens and even a few politicians were heard to worry aloud that it might be better to let "a few" people die rather than suffer such economic losses.

On March 27, 2020, Congress passed and the president signed the $2 trillion Coronavirus Aid, Relief, and Economic Security (CARES) Act, providing Economic Impact Payments to support American households, workers, small businesses, local governments, and industry. When it became clear that this bill would not be sufficient to cover the period of the virus, another bill passed the House, but the Senate refused to consider it. How was this money spent? A fair amount of it went to American households in a direct one-time dollar payment based on household incomes. Another substantial amount went to increase unemployment benefits for several months. Among the most needy and at-risk, however, both farmworkers and immigrant families in ICE centers (Immigration and Customs Enforcement) were not eligible for any assistance. And, while *Forbes* magazine reported on a "Greater Capitalism" that honors "a stakeholder economy" with "roots . . . in small businesses and entrepreneurs who ask for little more than a fair chance and a level playing field," in the same article, it also reported on a clumsy rollout of the CARES Act funding for "small businesses," in which "the first $350 billion tranche was gobbled up within days by the bigger, better-connected companies that knew how to play the game."[29] Apparently, this happened because the Small Business Administration's electronic system was directed to administer the funds, and many businesses, especially minority-owned ones, were unable to access that system.[30] In addition, Senate Republicans inserted into the CARES bill a $90 billion tax cut, whose benefits went primarily to those making over $1 million a year.[31] Data is not available for where all the money went, but evidence exists that another portion of the funds, meant financially to shore up local schools, was largely assigned to private schools, based on a decision by the secretary of education.[32]

It soon became clear that some groups of citizens were hit much harder than others. Black, Hispanic, Native American, and Asian people were disproportionately sickened and died from COVID-19 and were also first to be unemployed. As data began to come in from over the country, it revealed that "US counties that are majority-black have three times the rate of infections and almost six times the rate of deaths as counties that are majority-white."[33] Lower-income workers of all races and ethnicities who were now considered "essential" were at a higher risk of contracting the virus. Low- and middle-income elders in nursing homes were dying at the highest rate, accounting for nearly a fifth of all US deaths. In effect, race and poverty were "preexisting conditions" for COVID-19. Community housing situations such as jails and immigrant detention centers were at far greater risk for the virus, but operators often denied the ability to do anything about it.[34]

While the official unemployment rate overall was calculated at around 13 percent, the rate was much higher for certain groups; for example, more than one in four young adult US workers became unemployed or underemployed.[35] The term "essential workers" began to circulate, describing workers on the front lines of health, transportation, farming, and even meat-packing, who were among the lowest-paid workers in general but were still required to come to work, and thus more likely to be exposed to the virus. Those individuals and families already living with food insecurity faced decisions whether to pay rent/mortgage or buy food. It seemed likely that more than eighteen million children were to be food-insecure.[36] Cumulatively, these reports about our country's responses to the pandemic are very discouraging, even heartbreaking, at the blatant evidence of narcissism, greed, and lack of concern for our neighbors and the common good. We have been told many times that the American spirit is generous, especially in times of crisis. And yet in the light of the 2020 pandemic, there is remarkably little large-scale evidence of those qualities on which we so often pride ourselves.

Another disturbing fact about our American response to the virus was that many public and political figures, especially on social media, alleged that the publicity about COVID-19 was in fact a hoax or a conspiracy designed to erode the individual freedom at the heart of our democracy.[37] Whether or not to wear a mask in public became a political issue, and sheltering in place became tedious. The president warned that it would be terrible for the economy if the country stayed closed, and after a brief period, many Americans became angry that their state governments were "infringing on their freedom" to go out to restaurants and shops. While scientists argued that the best way to defeat the virus was to lower the curve, that is, to drive down the rate of viral transmission by staying at home, Americans often argued back that any so-called scientific fact was debatable. The "American way" seemed to be "to defend our freedoms fiercely, . . . bark in the face of fear, and we don't like being told what to do."[38] At least, these voices seemed to be the loudest at the moment.

Two dramatic and decisive events happened on May 25, 2020. That was Memorial Day in the US, a day when Americans traditionally have held an outdoor barbecue or beach party with family and friends. Many Americans felt they had been sheltered at home too long, and it was time to break out in celebration. Beaches and backyards all over the country became gathering places and few people wore masks or any protective equipment. In itself, that might have been enough to drive up cases of COVID-19, but something of even more importance to the country also happened that day. In Minneapolis, Minnesota, an assertive cop arrested a Black man named George Floyd for allegedly passing a counterfeit bill, and in a scuffle to get him into the police car, he was jammed onto the ground while the policeman pushed his leg into Floyd's neck for nine minutes and twenty-nine seconds until he died. A passerby filmed the event on a mobile phone, and within minutes it went viral. It was the third such unnecessary police action in the recent few months that resulted in death. And during the following week, America took to the streets in protest. Not only Black people but many Whites declared "Enough!" And not only Americans, but people worldwide marched in mostly peaceful protest against police brutality.

A *New York Times* article laid it out starkly: "There are parallel plagues ravaging America: the coronavirus. And police killings of black men and women."[39] Brad Braxton wrote in *The Christian Century* that he was saddened but not surprised by Floyd's death and others, because aggression against Black people seems woven into the myth of America. He urged that we hold a space for healing and lament, "because there remains somewhere in us a faint hope that today's pain will not completely swallow tomorrow's possibilities."[40]

As in the crisis of the 9/11 attacks on America, the coronavirus and the police killing of George Floyd were potential wake-up calls to our country. The loss of life in all cases was harrowing. Yet there is also a gift in a wake-up call, the invitation to become more self- and other-aware. We are called again to serious self-criticism, to ask honestly, what has our country become, how can we return to our beginnings, and how can we newly aspire to the ideal that every single being on our planet is entitled to respect and mutual care. Yet again, we slipped into the morass of denial. We refused the sacred opportunity.

The Role of Denial on the Way to Fullness of Life

In contemporary America, many of us find ourselves in twelve-step groups or psychological counseling, where the term "denial" often surfaces. Those of us familiar with the term and its role in psychological and spiritual health recognize that when we humans are faced with the "unthinkable," whether in public or private life, an initial reaction is often that of denial. When anything we encounter is terrible enough, it is human to stuff it away into an imaginary, seldom-used closet, and lock the door tightly. Some part of us feels that if we directly face something unthinkable or terrible, it will overwhelm us. We tend to think it will be more than we can handle, and facing it involves unacceptable risk. Yet strangely enough, life keeps presenting opportunities, even invitations, to unlock and open that mysterious and frightening door that we would rather ignore.

At a March 2020 virtual conference of spiritual directors (companions who help others deepen their spiritual life) convened to discuss the COVID-19 pandemic, members suggested that what seemed most frequently to surface in light of the coronavirus is *fear and a sense of vulnerability.* "The weight in this time is mainly a sense of fear and lack of clarity about a completely unknown future."[41] One's future seems dark, opaque, even cut off—this coronavirus is so new that one doesn't know when or how it might end, what to do to contain it, or what will happen to "normal" daily interactions. The coronavirus has revealed how much we depend upon tomorrow being like today, upon being able to "plan ahead." On the contrary, people like spiritual directors or psychologists and their clients, or like faithful twelve-step members, have discovered over time that darkness, when accompanied with compassion, can be a rich field for personal growth. "The invitation of darkness or fear is to lean in and embrace it, rather than to run away."[42] Very often, what has been hidden in a remote closet is exactly what carries the awareness necessary for our healing and wholeness.

For example, alcoholics very often become experts at denying they have a drinking problem. Generally speaking, one turns to alcohol to mask or numb some form of suffering or loss. Denial seems to arise from a sense of "caughtness," somewhat like the feeling of a youngster when caught in the very position of having a hand in the forbidden cookie jar. Often depression is a companion of alcoholism, a sense of emptiness or loneliness, a feeling that something is missing. There may even be a sense of shame that one needs the support or release alcohol can bring temporarily. Yet many recovering alcoholics have discovered a brand-new freedom of life when no longer in the grip either of the alcohol or of the underlying suffering. We see here what denial often masks: denial may be a useful mechanism early on when suffering is acute, but over time it is likely to block the way toward rediscovery of what needs to be integrated to bring wholeness of life.

While alcoholism has given us the language of denial, the growth of a variety of twelve-step groups has revealed the extent to which denial can become a problem in many human situations. These ideas become particularly relevant socially and politically in light of a powerful book written in 1973, a Pulitzer Prize winner by Ernest Becker, called *The Denial of Death*. Becker's well-researched thesis is that, since the human being is the only creature with the capacity to look ahead and know that he or she *will die*, the fear of death "haunts the human animal like nothing else."[43] The irony of human life is that on one hand, humans are symbolic, meaning that we can speculate about atoms and infinity or imagine ourselves in space looking back on the earth, but on the other hand, we are also assuredly still animals, when we die "going back into the ground a few feet in order blindly and dumbly to rot and disappear forever."[44] Becker, a psychologist post-Freud, knows all about the way humans can repress things they don't want to deal with, and he believes that most of the time, most of us repress our fear of death. In plain-spoken language, Becker asserts that humans are "gods who shit."[45]

Thirty years after Becker wrote his famous book, three of his previous students joined in another research project, exploring the possibility that not only do humans individually repress the fear of death, but that humans in community manage their fear of death by constructing and maintaining "a culturally derived worldview that imbues reality with order, stability, meaning, and permanence."[46] Such cultural world-views eventually become very powerful, and when individuals feel part of them, they contribute to a (distorted) sense of permanent reality that is used culturally to repress the fear of death at large. Hence, any perceived challenge to such a cultural worldview evokes and revives an immediate terror of death that the cultural worldview has effectively hidden from itself.

Becker's three colleagues developed what they call "Terror Management Theory," which they subsequently applied to the attacks of 9/11. They describe the immediate cultural reactions as predictably being disbelief, distraction,[47] drug and alcohol abuse, shunning large crowds as if potential targets of another attack, sacrificing some freedoms for heightened security, and intensifying bigotry. They further suggest that a longer-term issue is that the "mere existence of those who are different poses a threat to the individual's faith in the absolute validity and correctness of his or her own perspective on reality."[48] In the case of the 9/11 attacks, it was obvious that the cultural worldview of Islam and that of mainly Christian America heightened existing conflicts. But the opportunity for a deeper and more humane mutual understanding was cut off early on, rather than face either our fear or an inadequacy in our own viewpoint.

What I have tried to suggest in this chapter is that events such as the 9/11 attacks on America and the continuing threat of the coronavirus *both offered* our country an opportunity for critical self-examination of who we are today. Serious self-examination would involve (1) the need to re-member who we said we were in our founding as a country, (2) as well as finding psychological and political freedom to move on from "memories" cherished in a de-formed cultural worldview (3) toward new opportunities for ethical renewal. I believe we Americans have wrapped our political self-identity in a cultural worldview that no longer accurately describes us, and therefore needs to be re-visioned in light of the sacred. Our actual communal past may be experienced as impossible to accept or reconcile because it reveals wounds and scars that we have caused in our patriotic blindness. The increasingly obvious fact in a global world of others who are quite different from ourselves forces the admission that our "collective identity is rooted in founding events which are violent events. . . . A founding event in one group's collective memory may be a wound in the memory of the other."[49]

It may help to remind ourselves that, even while Israel suffered the great tragedy of exile, just as we are now suffering the great tragedy of sickness and death, Israel "clung to their status as exceptional people. They assumed that their exceptionalism was an earned status, when it was actually an endowed status by God."[50] In some ways, Americans are an exceptional people, and in some ways, we are quite ordinary and even cruel. And denial of our full humanness is a strategy with dangerous consequences, for it not only covers up old wounds but also covers up our only real opportunities for renewal and wholeness.

This concludes section I of this book, reviewing America's promise and our current inability to live into its challenging fruits. Section II will now lay out some of the realities America has ignored and denied, and that have defaced our once shining promise. I urge that we must face this de-formation today, if we seek to reclaim the promise of America. Our first task in the work of prophetic imagination is to see clearly, to witness honestly, to give up denial in order to see who we really are. Such witness must precede any serious efforts to find our way again. Section III will later demonstrate ways spiritual formation can and will strengthen and prepare us to challenge corrosive public policies, and thereby reclaim our country's promise.

Interlude A

Imperial Consciousness and Prophetic Imagination: Moses' Story

Benedict returns again and again to the question, "What does it mean to live as God would have us, in times like these?" I hope that question speaks not only to Americans who affirm one of the Abrahamic religions, but also the many religious traditions that aim for a more ethical and compassionate cultural and political worldview. Specifically, to address Benedict's ongoing query, here I will use Rowan Williams question, *how can we humans sustain a civilization capable of asking itself questions about its purpose and integrity?*

In order to present possibilities for a political role for the sacred in America (challenge), we need to have in mind and heart an honest assessment of what our times are like (witness). Section II next asks questions about America's purpose and integrity in light of our current policies with regard to four crucial matters, each of which has a separate chapter. Before looking specifically at the ways American public life is being de-formed by those four issues, however, it is valuable to have a fresh sense of Walter Brueggemann's distinction between royal/imperial consciousness and prophetic imagination in his book *The Prophetic Imagination*.

To help us understand his powerful metaphor of the difference between imperial consciousness and prophetic imagination, Brueggemann offers the biblical example of Moses' experience in Pharaoh's Egypt, when the suffering Hebrew people were treated as slaves. The prophetic ministry of Moses is able to create a radical break in Egypt's social reality, because Egypt at the time of the Hebrews' escape is clearly an example of royal or imperial consciousness. Any imperial regime will adopt "characteristic, recurring practices that serve to 'totalize' the claim of the regime, taking up all the social space, and allowing for no alternative possibility."[1] The gods of Egypt were the immovable lords of order, meaning that every political and economic arrangement, even those for religious and social practices, was designed to support Pharoah's order and to enforce his rule.[2] Any such dominating order is what Brueggemann calls royal consciousness, a pattern carefully designed to support the existing reign and punish any challenge to its political, economic, and/or religious arrangements. The Egyptian religion at that time was one of static triumphalism, and its politics were those of oppression and exploitation of its own people and certainly of its alien residents, the Hebrews.[3] How could such an oppressive and totalizing royal order be changed? The answer Brueggemann finds in Scripture is meaningful for us.

Those familiar with the biblical story know that Moses himself, though born a Hebrew, was raised as the adopted son of an Egyptian princess. He was reared in the midst of plenty and power, while the Hebrew people were enslaved, assigned to the lowest tasks, and living in poverty. Yet as a young man, Moses' anger was kindled and his heart broken when he saw one of his own Hebrew people being treated brutally. Taking things into his own hands, he killed the cruel overseer. However, someone saw Moses' act and threatened to report it, so Moses fled into the desert to a place called Midian, where he joined a community of distantly related people (offspring of Abraham), married, and became a shepherd. When years later Yahweh appeared to Moses, calling him to return and free the Hebrews from the Egyptian yoke, Moses nearly refused, because he well knew his personal inability to change royal control.

But the difference between this moment of call and Moses' previous action was that the free God Yahweh, whom Moses had come to know well in the simplicity of his desert life, was not constrained by the oppression of the Egyptian royal consciousness. Furthermore, Yahweh promised to go back to Egypt with Moses and his brother Aaron. Hence, in his return to Egypt, Moses now brought to the situation not only a refreshing politics of justice and compassion, but also the pivotal "disclosure of *the alternative religion of the freedom of God. . . .* Yahweh is extrapolated from no social reality and is captive to no social perception but acts from his own person toward his own purposes."[4]

Although the freeing of the Hebrew slaves is a major event of biblical history, more important than the event itself for Brueggemann is Moses' ability to break the chokehold that any royal/imperial consciousness claims over its society. Moses was filled with God's guidance and freedom, and thus able to "dismantle the (Egyptian) empire both in its social practices and in its mythic pretensions."[5] The point is that, subject to the overwhelming power and influence of royal/imperial consciousness, any energy emerging solely from the citizen-slaves, even working together, was not powerful enough to create major change, absent the presence and action of the free God. In these terms Brueggemann uses, it could equally be said that *our contemporary imperial America* intentionally produces a form of consciousness that creates personal despair, numbs citizens' feelings and motives, and weakens energy for renewal, *in the absence of a meaningful role for the sacred.*

Brueggemann describes the task Moses accepted as the work of prophetic imagination. This task involves joining God in providing energy for hope, cutting through social numbness, and penetrating the cultural self-deception of royal/imperial consciousness, in order that God and the sacred again become visible and energizing for the people.[6] This work, which I believe calls us Americans today no less than it called Moses centuries ago, has three basic parts:

(1) to offer symbols reactivated out of the people's past, powerful enough to confront the horror and massiveness of imperial dealings;

(2) to bring "to public expression the very fears and terrors, as well as the hopes and yearnings, that have been denied so long and suppressed so deeply that we do not know they are there"[7]; and

(3) to speak "metaphorically but concretely about the real deathliness that hovers over us and gnaws within us," speaking neither in rage nor with cheap grace, but "with the candor born of anguish and passion."[8]

Imperial consciousness is powerful, and prophetic imagination is hard work on many levels. Yet I write to encourage you to take up these tasks, because I firmly believe (a) that it is not too late to shift course, (b) that our country is still a democracy in which the cumulative voice of the people can make a substantial difference, and (c) that calling upon Spirit for help brings additional resources to the table. Section II lays out in detail the de-forming patterns of America's present "imperial consciousness" in order that we can witness it clearly. It is subtitled "the pathos of God" because when we witness and grieve the state of our country in times like these, we also experience God's empowering grief and receive the ability to respond effectively to God's call to possible futures.

Section II

Witness to De-Formation: The Pathos of God

CHAPTER THREE

Uncritical Confidence in Market Culture

> *Alas for those who devise wickedness*
> *and evil deeds . . .*
> *[and] perform it,*
> *because it is in their power.*
> *They covet fields, and seize them;*
> *houses, and take them away;*
> *they oppress householder and house,*
> *people and their inheritance. . . .*
> *[They say,] "disgrace will not overtake us." . . .*
> *And I said:*
> *Listen, you heads of Jacob*
> *and rulers of the house of Israel!*
> *Should you not know justice?* (Mic 2:1-2, 6b, 3:1)

Section II of this book returns to Rowan Williams's important question, *how can we humans sustain a civilization capable of asking itself questions about its purpose and integrity?*

The whole of section II asks that question about the present condition of American public affairs, especially with regard to four patterns currently denominating our national life: (1) uncritical confidence in market culture, (2) overweening growth in our global empire, (3) denial of Earth's climate crisis, and (4) resistance to diversity. The work of this section is to make radically visible what I call the imperial consciousness that now dominates our national life. The detail provided about each of these de-forming patterns is intended to break through our denial of their significance. We all probably have some sense of these four issues in our midst. However, partly because each pattern is wrapped in some secrecy but also partly because their reality and pervasiveness is so "unthinkable," we are prone to dismiss and discount how severely they now dominate our life together. In effect, God's sacred invitations to us are muffled by the imperial consciousness surrounding our lives.

This section is crucial to the first step of what Brueggemann has called prophetic imagination, to clear away the lies of imperial consciousness in contemporary America. In order to move forward toward effective challenge to that smoky imperial screen, we must first be clear about what we witness. The work of thorough self-examination requires that we lay out directly the extent to which the US has ignored or hidden specific policies that today cause worldwide suffering. It is not easy to speak nor to read about these matters, but I do speak and urge you to continue reading. This section is called "the pathos of God" because when we see clearly enough to grieve the state of our country in times like these, we are experiencing God's grief, which will guide and govern our own.

Market Culture at Home

In chapter 3, we begin with an in-depth look at market culture as it presently operates in America. The term "market culture" is a relatively new one, but the experience is fairly common today. Alain Richard, OFM, proposes that a new cultural worldview has been birthed from the womb of the market, "suffocating the values rooted in the Greco-Latin and Judeo-Christian human-centered visions of life."[1] Although the term "market culture" refers in part to consumerism, its larger meaning refers to the *substitution of moral principles by other principles* established for the material success of the market system.

The time is past when an employee might work for the same company for a lifetime, because now corporations cite competition and other dangers to their survival in order to justify selling or relocating factories where cheaper labor is available. The health care system is largely governed by financial managers, so the first question when one seeks medical care is not about one's name, but whether one has insurance; and then office visits are limited by the same financial managers to fifteen minutes. Universities advertise themselves as the best place to prepare for certain jobs, rather than places to learn history and ethics. In a "whistle-blower" account of the social media giant Facebook, Frances Haugen provided information to *The Wall Street Journal* and testified to a US Senate committee that not only is Facebook "wired to fuel and feed off rage" but it also harms children, with its Instagram program "leading them to anorexia-related content." Summarizing her concerns, Haugen claims that "the company puts profit over people's safety."[2] In the US, even electoral politics has been assimilated to the principles of the market, with candidates as products sold by slogans and advertisements.[3] Theologian John Cobb observes that "economic theory has become the basic theology of the world."[4] In other words, Money and Profit are now God.

The secular language of economics has frequently borrowed fundamentalist religious language to justify its increasing dominance. Referring back to seventeenth-century English liberalism while narrowing its sense of care for people, human beings are now viewed as "autonomous rational subjects who act solely to maximize individual self-interest."[5] In this way of thinking, wealth is equated with happiness, and Earth sets no intrinsic limits to endless growth and maximization of wealth. This view is rooted in several dogmas: (1) economic growth benefits all humans, (2) market freedom is equated with human freedom and democracy, and (3) this system is natural, normative, and inevitable, built into the very nature of things. Despite on-the-ground evidence that these dogmas are seldom true, this "secular religion" has become normative for America's political and economic leadership.[6] In fact, Brueggemann has called market ideology "our specific form of totalism" (imperial consciousness) and warns that its outcome is "the monetizing of all social relationships, the commoditization of all social possibilities, and the endless production of dispensable persons."[7]

Fr. Richard offers a helpful list that I have prepared in chart form, comparing what he calls market culture and human-based culture.[8] It is described narratively below the chart.

Chart Comparison of Market Culture and Human-Based Culture

Activity	Market Culture	Human-Based Culture
Goal	making a profit, economic prosperity	honoring the dignity of every person and valuing holistic societies
Work	making money, production for its own sake	producing necessities, expressing one's gifts, contributing to society
Workers	producers and consumers	involved in a dynamic web of relationships to build capacities to love and be loved
Society	limit intrusion of others upon an individual's rights	all persons strengthened and united in the common good
Relationships	utilitarian, competitive, victory to the strongest	a sense of reverence and respect for the sacred within all

In general, market culture has become so pervasive that we hardly notice the considerable shift from the human-based values to market-based values, yet, as we see them laid out, right away we recognize the market values. Indeed, the human-based values seem almost starry-eyed, well beyond the bounds of possibility. We notice exactly what imperial consciousness has promised, a way of thinking that encompasses everything in its scope; it totalizes all and makes anything different seem impossible. We will see this again and again as we consider these four de-forming practices. In order to challenge our initial reaction of incredulity that these so-called human-based values could even be feasible, let's take some time with each of them, in contrast to existing market culture.

First, the goal of market culture is material development and economic prosperity, compared to a human-based culture's goal as the holistic development of human beings and their societies. How often have we heard someone say, "I took the better-paying job but I hate every minute of it!" How seldom do we hear someone say, "I feel my work helps me be a better human being." The second aspect of market culture is that work itself is seldom seen as a means to care for one's family and/or express one's gifts. Commonly in market culture, work is a means of making money, producing things that are not necessary for human life, but which are advertised as (luxury) items that no "ordinary household" can do without. Comparatively, in a human-based culture, work does provide necessities but also is a means by which a person expresses their particular gifts, thereby contributing to society. Wendell Berry makes this point painfully in his opposition to the frequent opinion that it is a good thing for farm families to "leave the burden" of daily work in maintaining the farm (thus making their days full of family life together) so that they can "earn money" in outside paid jobs.⁹ Berry knows that farm work is hard and sometimes harsh, but he also knows the satisfaction that comes from "doing for one's family."

The third issue in market culture is that workers are treated primarily as producers and consumers, useful as long as they are able to fulfill a specific function, but to whom the employer has no long- or even short-term personal obligation. In contrast, a human-based culture views the worker in a dynamic web of relationships through which he or she becomes a complete person. During the pandemic, many workers were abruptly fired, with no consideration of a possible return when the pandemic eased. Hence, the health problem immediately became an employment problem, in which some employers moved to other locations where they could hire cheaper labor, rather than become engaged with families of workers to help them withstand the crisis. Meanwhile, the better-off members of society were tempted to make critical comments about "lazy" people who preferred a government subsidy rather than do "honest work" for long hours at low wages. In a market-based culture, neither employers nor employees are aided to become more mature.

Fourth, society in a market culture is simply the sum of individual decisions, which the market endeavors to influence by artificially creating ever-expanding needs and wants. I've often thought that one of the things that market culture has learned to do very well is to advertise. Would young people want so urgently to smoke cigarettes and drink beer if they were not bombarded with advertisements about "the good life" filled with happy people smoking and drinking? Why do we not see this and express concern? Indeed, imperial consciousness has us well in hand. In a human-based society, each person's life is strengthened by a sense of the common good, to which each contributes and from which each benefits. Within today's individualism, we hardly have a sense of anything like the common good.

Fifth, and finally, relationships in the market culture are utilitarian, whereas in a human-based culture, every being is viewed with respect and reverence as bearing a spark of sacred presence.[10] In short, in market culture, everything (including persons) becomes a product, to be valued only so long as it is useful, obtained at the cheapest possible price and sold whenever a better price is available. Even if our own immediate families care for us, it is mightily discouraging to realize that the culture at large views us only in terms of how useful we are, which often leads in turn to feeling we must be useful or we have no value. And, of course, the implication of the market view is that the wealthy are nearly gods, and the poor are disposable. Community is inconceivable. And, as Richard points out in the title of his book, violence is a frequent outcome in such a culture.

One of the primary reasons for the power of the market culture in the US today is that it finds its justification and attractiveness in what might be called the "American dream." Almost from its beginnings, the US has cast the allure that in this country, anyone can "make it big." No matter how poor to start with, anyone willing to work hard can buy a fancy car, have a lovely home, and make lots of money. It is doubtful that dream was ever realistic, although many of us can tell a story of one person who has putatively gone from rags to riches. It is certainly no longer true that anyone can do so, except in very rare instances.

In fact, one of the commonly posed questions to demonstrate how personal wealth has no limits is currently backfiring. The question is "Do you earn more than your parents did at the same age?" The answer is "yes" for 92 percent of Americans born around 1940. However, many Americans born in 1980 and since have had difficulty making even 50 percent of what their parents did at their age. And the disparities of wealth are far greater than those of income. Of the $67 trillion of US family wealth in 2013, 76 percent of that wealth belonged to the top 10 percent, whose wealth average was $4 million. In contrast, the *bottom half* of the US population receives only one percent of the total. Those in the 26th to 50th percentiles averaged just $36,000 in total family wealth, an amount that would barely buy a new mid-range automobile. And the bottom quarter of the population had negative wealth; that is, they *owed* an average of $13,000 per family.[11] And these disparities increase.

Even though stock prices have consistently been in a bull market in recent years, most Americans own little or no stock; they are lucky to own their own home. *The New York Times* reports, "Living the American dream is now akin to a coin flip."[12] Inequality of incomes within the US has soared over the past forty-plus years. The richest 0.1 percent now have the same combined net worth as the bottom 85 percent.[13] If we distinguish between White persons having a four-year college degree and Whites who do not, the White working class is the largest demographic in the US, with 42 percent of Americans in this category. However, they are *not* a largely rural, monolithic group; 62 million of them live within the larger environs of cities of more than 250,000 inhabitants. And they are all too aware of the effects of changing economic data on their lives. Tex Sample, an author specializing in church and society, and the Robert B. and Kathleen Rogers Professor Emeritus of Church and Society at the St. Paul School of Theology, has wisely taken on the task of understanding who the members of the White working class are, while dispelling some of the biases that have crept into public thought.[14]

Meanwhile, the four top internet industries, Facebook, Amazon, Apple, and Google, are now jointly worth nearly *five trillion dollars* and make up 22 percent of the entire S&P 500 of the American stock market. In July 2020, their respective CEOs were called to testify before the congressional House Judiciary Subcommittee on Antitrust Law regarding possible antitrust violations. Each of the CEOs denied any illegal actions, explaining that any market control they do exert "is simply American."[15] Simply American! If you doubt that money and profit have become God in America, note this defense well! Even so, the American dream continues to enchant most of us and partially justify such shocking discrepancies in wealth.

The Greek root of the word "economy" is *oikonomia*, whose meaning was originally the art of managing a household, and later came to refer to the method of *divine* government of the world, though the contemporary meaning actually is far removed from anything hands on. Today, the term "economy" refers to the use of money to make money, largely by transnational corporations, "emphasizing cash management and its profitability over the traditional commitment to manufacture a product."[16] In other words, frequently today money is invested not with a plan to create needed goods, but instead with a plan to make more money. An early example is that of the Lykes Corporation, which purchased Youngstown Sheet and Tube in Ohio to use the steel company as a "cash cow," milking it for high profits that provided capital for investment elsewhere, only to close it a few years later with no concern for local workers. This shift in understanding represents a marked departure from a centuries-long concept of money. Initially money was an invention designed to replace the barter system. (For example, I'll give you three chickens for one pig.) Instead, today using money to make money often disconnects the entire process from real-world transactions.

There is only so much data that the human mind can absorb. So, please take a break if you need to, then return to this next section. Realistically, we cannot be adequately prepared to take back our people's own democratic accountability and leadership until we gain an integrated sense of the full implications of our distorted worship of wealth. The data above suggest how much household suffering is caused within our homeland by these economic realities. Our vision of market culture is only partial, however, until we also take an unblinkered look at the worldwide effects of our American reliance on a market culture that shapes our values and policy decisions.

Market Culture Worldwide:
The Bretton Woods Institutions

At the end of World War II, recognizing the growing interrelationship of nations, the Allied nations planned to create an improved international order. The first steps were to create the United Nations as a political institution, and the World Bank and the International Monetary Fund as international economic institutions. The latter two, along with the World Trade Organization created somewhat later, were collectively referred to as the Bretton Woods Institutions. Both England and France had been devastated by their losses in the war, as had Russia to some extent, and thus it seemed logical for the US to play a major role in these new international organizations. As a result, both the International Monetary Fund and the World Bank were located in Washington, DC. As long as the Soviet Union remained a strong communist presence, US foreign policy was focused on "keeping as many third-world countries as possible on the American side of the Cold War."[17] With the Marshall Plan in place to support Europe and Robert McNamara at the head of the World Bank, American leadership and the American people generally seemed to be working from humanitarian sentiments both at home and abroad.

Initially the World Bank sought to reduce poverty in Europe and the southern hemisphere, but two problems developed. The bank's preferred modes of development were to push high-volume, low-interest development loans and to build dams, especially in the poorer countries. However, the dams often displaced many people without appropriate resettlement, and many families who had survived by farming or fishing found their livelihoods destroyed, while any environmental devastation was largely ignored.[18] The second initial problem was that, given the rules under which loans were made to needy countries, the money often went no further than local elites. "Third world countries mostly produced commodities, while they had to import machinery and other high-tech goods. The price of what they imported went up, and the price of what they exported went down," while discontent built up.[19]

Matters boiled into a crisis in 1982, when Mexico announced it could not pay its debts and proposed to take bankruptcy, causing the international economic institutions to fear a broader renunciation of debts by poorer nations. The US government brought everyone together for renegotiations, so that Mexico need not go bankrupt. A concept called "structural adjustment" was put into play by the banks, "billed as 'austerity' measures that would cause 'temporary pain' (to whom?)

but would soon cause the whole local economy to adjust and prosper."[20] The intention was initially described as helping to make sure that local elites could not hoard the loaned money and the benefits would actually reach the poor.

These were the requirements of structural adjustment. First, the local currency was devalued. Second, interest rates on loans rose sharply. Third, trade barriers that had protected local industries and agriculture were removed, allowing international corporations essentially to control local development. Fourth, enterprises such as transportation, energy, telephones, electricity, and even water supply—traditionally made available as public services—were privatized, also allowing purchase by international corporations. Fifth, minimum wage laws and state subsidies for education and health care were disallowed. And finally, each country was required to focus on one or two traditional export commodities like coffee or sugar to repay debts, "at the expense of the diversification of agricultural and industrial production for local consumption."[21] That last requirement meant, of course, that family farms could no longer support themselves from their own land.

Please reread and take a little time with this list above. A first thought is that the US would never allow any external institution to take over that much control of our economy. The insistence that small and poor nations give up control of their own resources is clearly meant to humiliate them on the world stage, quite apart from the fact of using them as "cash cows," as mentioned earlier about the steel company in Ohio. It is obvious that such bank requirements not only cause incredible harm to the environment, but primarily cause suffering to the world's poor. This is an explicit formula for making sure that the rich get richer and the poor get poorer. The rationale rests on an "economic theory, which prizes private ownership and free competition above all else."[22] The underlying principles of this economic theory are that any business owned by government should be privatized (even made available for sale to companies with no loyalty to the local country); any government regulation is always bad (as Catholic theologian and world-renowned eco-feminist scholar Rosemary Ruether asks, for whom?); and after all, the market always operates fairly ("the standard formula is that a willing seller sold to a willing buyer").

It has long been clear that this economic theory has little or no basis in fact, especially when expected to function in the market complexity of what is now a global economy. While the intention was initially framed as a desire to create a level playing field throughout the world, the rules governing structural adjustment were not equally applied to rich nations, so the global playing field has remained noticeably uneven. The US and Europe continued to subsidize our own agricultural production, making our surplus production cheap on the world market, with the result that "peasants in poor countries have to compete, without subsidies or tariff protection, with highly subsidized American agribusiness."[23]

Despite all this, the Bretton Woods Institutions continued to impose their structural adjustment policies on other countries throughout the world. "Structural Adjustment has had the effect of *creating a net extraction of wealth from poor to rich countries*, or rather, to international banks. For example, in 1988, $50 billion more was paid by poor countries to banks than were actually loaned to them from banks."[24] And these economic institutional requirements were joined to various tariff controls, intensifying the extraction of wealth from poor countries. Initially tariffs were controlled by the World Trade Organization, and when these failed to increase profits enough to satisfy international corporations, other constraints were added, as for example by NAFTA, the North American Free Trade Agreement, which, among its other provisions, *allows a corporation to sue a nation for loss of projected profits if governments pass labor or environmental laws!* Again, dear reader, listen twice, take this in, and acknowledge how different these regulations are from a sense of responsibility for the common good. You may wish to ask me why I quote so confidently from John Cobb and Rosemary Ruether. Who are they and can we trust their insights? Both are dedicated Christians and teachers at Christian seminaries. While their books were not written recently, our American submission to the dominant imperial consciousness has meant that neither of these books received the attention they should have, at the time. Yet Cobb and Ruether are intelligent and trustworthy people, and their insights remain significant. My prayer is that this time around, we will pay attention.

It has become increasingly clear that the policies of the Bretton Woods Institutions, directed by US advisors, are closely linked to US commercial interests, particularly those of multinational corporations. "The third world has been reorganized for the sake of increasing subservience to Washington and for repayment of debts to the first world."[25] Why does the third world consent? Ruether suggests three reasons: first, wealthy elites and local dictators are still prospering; second, third world economists were trained in the same schools of economics and accepted their economic theories as dogma; and third, any governments that resisted would be scorned, isolated, and refused further assistance.[26] On-the-ground resistance does continue, as, for example, in peasant and church resistance in Latin America, but the US has repeatedly intervened to squash such resistance, sometimes directly with our own troops, and sometimes through local military forces. And places like the Western Hemisphere Institute for Security Cooperation (WHINSEC), formerly known as the School of the Americas, a US Department of Defense institute located in Georgia, have actively trained troops from Latin America in what is called "low-intensity warfare," which includes torture.[27]

The World Trade Organization (WTO) was set up in the Uruguay round of the General Agreement on Tariffs and Trade (GATT), essentially as the executive and judicial arm of GATT, the international body negotiating "free trade" agreements worldwide. As with the other two Bretton Woods Institutions, initially the WTO received little public attention, appearing to be rather technical and boring. In effect, however, "WTO became an agency of global corporate rule with the power to override national laws."[28] Rulings of the WTO tribunals are made by an unelected group of bureaucrats in closed door proceedings in Geneva, whose procedures are secret and documents are confidential. The WTO decisions even *prevent* the US from banning gas that contains unsafe additives, *prevent* the European Union from banning hormones in beef, and *prevent* African governments from obtaining less expensive AIDS drugs to supply their people. Various interest groups began to form to contest these inhumane and dangerous economic policies, such as the World Social Forum, Non-Governmental Organizations (NGOs), church groups, unions, and the Direct Action Network.

Accountability at World Trade Organization Meetings

In 1999, a WTO meeting was scheduled in Seattle, planning to launch a new Millennial Round of trade negotiations, expanding the right of corporations to sue governments for such things as loss of potential profits due to, say, government bans on unsafe additives in gasoline. The Direct Action Network and others experienced in nonviolent protests gathered upwards of sixty thousand people to protest the meeting and the agenda.[29] Most of those who attended had participated in days and weeks of nonviolence training and jail training in order to understand what might happen, had signed nonviolence agreements, and were placed together in small groups called "affinity groups," each with leaders trained to assess what was happening in their immediate area and to make adjustments to maximize flexibility, minimize violence, and keep people safe as possible. They were also committed to include in their action art, dance, song, and a celebration of creativity and connection. Their longer-term goal was to "build a global movement to overthrow corporate control and to create a new economy based on fairness and justice, on a sound ecology and a healthy environment, one that protects human rights and serves freedom."[30]

The protesters blockaded the entrance to the building, so members of the WTO could not enter, and the opening meeting was shut down. The police were unprepared for the large numbers of protestors, however, and they reacted with violence. Both sides were fearful, and media reports emphasized the violence, with little comprehension of the aims and commitments of nonviolent protest (even though it is a legal option in the US, and even though Gandhiji and the Rev. Dr. Martin Luther King Jr. had long since demonstrated its motives and strategies). Also, America itself has a strong history of direct action-oriented social movements rooted in spirituality, led, for example, by Quaker abolitionists, church leaders, unions, Indigenous groups, Black civil rights activists, and others.

Citizens choose nonviolent protest *only* when they believe first, that something important is at stake, and second, that there is no other way for their voices to be heard. Even in a putative democracy, when excessively expensive political campaigns often result in choices at the ballot box that are no choice at all, alternatives are limited. When president after president continues to support the Bretton Woods Institutions, how can the public have an effective voice? When basic communication has been ignored or disregarded for a long time, and when the system in place ignores talk and responds with state-sponsored violence to repeated and urgent concerns, the options are limited: first, to keep things the same, while possibly taking out our rage on those closest to us and/or drifting into depression and apathy; second, to start a violent revolution; or third, to "mobilize our radical imagination, to create an alternative so inspiring and compelling that the masses of people who yearn for both freedom and abundance will join us."[31] Radical imagination is one of the essential ingredients in breaking through imperial consciousness. Genuine active nonviolence creates imaginative new possibilities. That is why a respected theologian like Walter Brueggemann calls not only for contemporary prophets, but for "imaginative prophecy."[32]

With its relative success in Seattle, the many groups committed to global justice decided to continue their direct action at subsequent meetings of the Bretton Woods Institutions and its leadership in Washington, DC, Prague, Brazil, Quebec City, and Genoa, each increasingly subject to police abuse and misinterpretation by the media, yet also successful in raising issues that otherwise generally were kept from public view.

The meeting in Genoa of the G8 leaders (the US, Canada, Great Britain, Germany, Italy, France, Japan, and Russia) occurred in July 2001, and the nonviolent action was organized by the Genoa Social Forum, a coalition of over seven hundred groups, NGOs, unions, and political parties, with people attending from over five countries. The Social Forum had been told that the Indy Media Center and Diaz School had been set aside as places for protesters to stay in sleeping bags and work on their computers. The first day began with generally peaceful street protests, until riot police arrived in the afternoon with tear gas and clubs, beating pacifists who approached with hands up, while helicopters buzzed overhead. Protesters returned to the convergence center, connecting with each other and trying to figure out what was going on. Suddenly, the police arrived, went into one of the two centers (where no one could get out because of a crush at the only door), and began going floor to floor, beating people up. In riot gear the police went into rooms where people were sleeping, viciously beating each person, breaking bones, smashing teeth, and shattering skulls. They wrecked computers and equipment, arrested everyone, including well over two dozen who were subsequently removed to the hospital. Initially, the media and politicians were kept out by a police cordon. Later the protesters learned that those taken to jail were tortured.

The police only left when officials from the Genoa Social Forum, some parliament members, and the media arrived. It was obvious that the police could openly carry out such brutal acts and falsely arrest even Italians *only* because they knew they had support from the highest levels and did not expect to be held accountable even to their own people. On Monday after the meeting, however, over 250,000 Italians took to the streets in protest, and demonstrations against the police violence took place in Italian embassies all over the world. Starhawk, who was there, writes that "Genoa was a painful, shattering, but also illuminating experience. . . . Fear is the most powerful weapon (of the oppressors). The fact that they must resort to fascist violence shows that we (the supporters of global justice) are a serious threat."[33]

Active nonviolence is not an easy nor comforting choice because the more committed the system is to its current policies, the more harshly it will react to the challenge of thousands of protesters. If protests are not influencing public opinion, no response at all need be made by the system. Only when direct action on the streets enlivens the imagination of a large public, only then does the system need to react with all the force at its power. Genoa is a horrifying example. The same result may not have happened in a nation less accustomed to state violence. But Genoa also reveals how seriously these economic decisions are held by those in power who make them. Direct action is not for all of us to do; however, those willing to undertake it are opening the door for many more of us desirous of deeper and more open discussion of alternatives to the present world order.

Challenge to These Signs of the Times

It is noteworthy that many powerful people are now and have for some time challenged these existing global economic policies. For example, Pope Francis has established a personal Council for Inclusive Capitalism, urging the promotion of a more just and humane economy. His first apostolic exhortation includes a chapter titled, "Amid the Crisis of Communal Commitment," in which he discusses the context in which we all live and work, exhorting a watchful scrutiny of the signs of the times. In light of "new and often anonymous kinds of power," the pope urges that collectively we say:

> No to an economy of exclusion . . . No to the new idolatry of money . . . No to a financial system which rules rather than serves . . . [and] No to the inequality which spawns violence.[34]

The pope elaborates his challenge to de-forming economic power as a symbol of "a rejection of ethics and a rejection of God. Ethics has come to be viewed with a certain scornful derision . . . because it makes money and power relative [by condemning] the manipulation and debasement of the person. In effect, ethics leads to a God who calls for a committed response which is *outside the categories of the marketplace*, [calling] human beings to their full realization."[35] The pope's powerfully articulated statement was quickly dismissed by reporter Matthew Lau of a Toronto newspaper, with the scornful amusement of people committed to the way things are. Lau, obviously using the economic standards preferred by the US corporate elite that have resulted in the gross disparities described above, claims that "in the Pope's world of alternative economics, it seems up is down, left is right, good is bad."[36] Perhaps Lau's economics are the upside-down ones.

A second strong challenge to current global economic policies comes from author Ched Myers, an activist theologian and director of Bartimaeus Cooperative Ministries, occasional contributor to *Sojourners* magazine, and popular educator throughout North America and internationally. Myers insists that "the standard of economic and social justice is woven into the warp and weft of the Bible, and at the heart of this witness is the call to observe Sabbath economics" in public and family settings. The biblical Sabbath Jubilee calls for regular and systematic wealth and power distribution, including release of slaves, deconstruction of debt, and return of foreclosed land, a call which Myers insists "is neither utopian nor abstract."[37] Myers challenges the contemporary economic policies of the US to follow three biblical axioms:

- The world as created by God is abundant, with enough for everyone—provided that human communities restrain their appetites and live within limits;

- Disparities in wealth and power are not "natural" but the result of human sin, and must be mitigated within the community of faith through the regular practice of redistribution; and

- The prophetic message calls people to the practice of such redistribution, and is thus characterized as "good news" to the poor.[38]

This is indeed a radical challenge and an imaginative yet possible alternative vision for contemporary America. It sounds strange to our ears because it is so greatly at odds with the governmental and economic priorities we live with. We do not need to be Jewish or Christian to take these axioms seriously, and to urge our leaders in this direction. In the context of this book's prophetic self-examination of where our culture is today, and of its urgent call for a role for the sacred in public policy, it is well worth remembering that whenever we hear ourselves saying or thinking, "That's impossible," it is time to pause and reconsider. The imperial consciousness has two major tools—to stunt our imagination and to flatten our affect, our ability to care and love.

CHAPTER FOUR

Overweening Growth in Our Global Empire

Therefore, thus says the Lord GOD to them: I myself will judge between the fat sheep and the lean sheep. Because you pushed with flank and shoulder, and butted at all the weak animals with your horns until you scattered them far and wide, I will save my flock, and they shall no longer be ravaged. (Ezek 34:20-22)

One of the primary tasks of the prophetic imagination to which we are called is to speak concretely about the real deathliness that hovers over us and gnaws within us. Chapter 3 took up that task with regard to the dominance of market culture in contemporary America, enabling market values, specifically profit-making, to overcome every other standard of value. Now chapter 4 takes up the second mode of deathliness that is de-forming our culture: the American global empire, constructed on the values of the market economy.

It will surprise no one that globalization is an increasingly important aspect of contemporary life. When the term is used merely to refer to the transcendence of earlier national and local limits, it is of course, morally and politically neutral. However, today globalization "exists as a particular mutant of postmodern capitalism, an attempt to impose the interests of wealthy power structures in the West upon the world. As such it is politically imperialistic, environmentally unsustainable, and morally questionable."[1] It is in this latter sense that the term "global" is used and discussed in this chapter.

"Empire" is the second term in the title of this chapter because that is what the US global strategy behaves like today. In the nineteenth century, the idea of American imperialism was freely discussed under the theory that, based on our founding documents affirming our "God-blessed" country, the US was a benign and even benevolent "empire of liberty."[2] For a time, vigorous debates were held over whether the term "empire" was appropriate for the US, because unlike Great Britain and other European countries in an earlier century, we did not (and do not) have formal colonies. Nonetheless, the ideology of empire is not conditioned on the possession of formal colonies, but rather "it expresses the desire to add to one's wealth and to dominate over others. . . . The ideology assumes that if one group is able to assert its will over others, then it is superior to them and has the right to exploit them."[3] The actual strength of empire may rest in economic and/or military presence (rather than political control), but imperial ideology always claims cultural and moral superiority, as well as an implicit racial superiority. Some commentators view empire as the primary and first organizing principle of the combined de-forming policies that these chapters describe, but I place market culture first as the primary organizing principle. I do so because I believe American empire tends, in all its forms, to *follow the profit.* That standard is visible in our consistent disregard for people located on the margins of society and for the increasing destruction of our resources. The decisions made at all levels of our global empire are based on maximizing profit. No allowance is made for compassion, for the sustainability of earth-based resources that our great-grandchildren will need, nor for however many deaths might be required to accomplish present purposes. Clearly, American empire itself is valued because market culture, greed, in fact, is its foundation. As seen earlier, money reveals itself as the god of empire who claims obedience.

Thomas Berry describes the development of modern American industrial, commercial, and financial corporations as intimately connected with our history—beginning with land corporations, chartered initially by England as the Virginia Company and the New England Company in the 1600s, distributing the vast lands of the new continent to individual persons such as William Penn. In 1812, the US Land Grant Office was established, at which time the federal government "owned 756 million acres of land," which was sold as a commodity to members of the public at minimal cost.[4] The second phase of US corporate development might be called the canal and railroad phase. Although lands for these uses were sold to private corporations, development was additionally subsidized by state governments. The third phase began after the Civil War, when private corporations were allowed to take over extraction of natural resources in mines, oil wells, steel furnaces, and building infrastructure. Each of these phases also came with some backlash, in growing concern about destruction of the natural environment, poor working conditions, and maldistribution of income. But little came of such concerns when Darwin's newly published theories about "survival of the fittest" so well suited American individualism and attachment to private property. Of course the "fittest" (which in America generally meant the richest) were intended to prosper. Meanwhile, the visible industrial-technological transformations of the times offered heady assurances that the public interest was being served.

A major step in corporate control of public policy occurred in 1886 when, with citizens presumably convinced that only corporate leadership could promise public well-being, US law was changed by the courts to label corporations "individuals." Hence corporations were able to resist government regulation while still managing to receive government subsidies in "thanks" for their ongoing contributions toward the public good. This outrageous fiction still exists, assuring that corporations continue to produce substantial dividends for shareholders, while paying workers minimal salaries.[5] As recently as

October 2020, David Leonhardt wrote in *The New York Times* that the overriding goal of corporate policy was to reduce corporate regulations and taxes, and to stop "confiscatory taxation" and intrusive "safety and health regulations."[6]

This background on corporate influences in the American global empire is necessary for a full understanding of the nature of our empire, which consists in three primary components: (1) worldwide financial strength, (2) the expansion of largely American-based multinational corporations, and (3) the extension of American military presence to support the other two. Our global role is guided by an American elite consisting of corporate directors, top politicians, and military chiefs, generally out of view of American citizens. Let's look at these three basic pillars as they support the US imperial stance. The first one, financial power, which has already been discussed in the previous chapter regarding the Bretton Woods Institutions, is briefly outlined below. The second pillar of the American empire is worldwide corporate dominance. And the third pillar is worldwide military power. The second and third pillars are the primary focus in this chapter.

Pillar 1:
Financial Power in Global Empire (Reminder)

The American global empire relies on the powers given to international corporations by the Bretton Woods Institutions (the World Bank, etc.) through their structural adjustment modifications. Remember that these institutions are largely home based in the US and have key representatives of the US elite on their boards of governance. Recall too that these banking rules have been imposed on poor countries as loan conditions, all favoring global corporate actors.

- Local currency was devalued.
- Trade barriers were removed from poor nations but retained by wealthy ones.

- Traditionally "public" industries—water, energy, trans-portation—were privatized and available *for sale* to transnational corporations.

- Minimum wage laws and state subsidies for education and health were disallowed.

- Small farms supporting owner families were forbidden to grow food for the family but required to grow traditional export commodities.

- And transnational corporations were allowed to *sue poor countries for potential loss of profits* caused by local environmental or other regulations.

Pillar 2:
Worldwide Corporate Domain of Global Empire

As an introduction to the role of corporations in our global empire, let's consider David Korten's distinction between characteristics of empire and those of his preferred model, called "earth community."[7]

Empire	Earth Community
Life is hostile and competitive	Life is supportive and cooperative
Humans are flawed/dangerous	Humans have many possibilities
Order by dominator hierarchy	Order through partnership
Compete or die	Cooperate and live
Love power	Love life
Defend the rights of oneself	Defend the rights of all
Masculine dominant	Gender balanced

As we saw in the chart in chapter 3, the items listed under empire are very familiar to us. We might use somewhat different terms, but basically we understand those characteristics for their familiarity in contemporary American culture. As noted above, the first listed quality of empire sounds very much like what we have understood from Darwin's theories about nature (hostile and competitive), while the idea that life could be supportive and cooperative sounds a bit like "pie in the sky." We are so accustomed to ordering things by hierarchy that the notion that order could actually be achieved by partnership seems to be just wishful thinking. The pandemic with the issues it has raised about masks and vaccinations has simply blossomed with cries that requirements like that interfere with primary individual rights, no matter that refusing them may cause others to die! Finally, we have lived so long with the notion of masculine dominance that many people still wonder whether women are even capable of doing difficult work. As before, we see that charts like this one reveal how profoundly we have allowed imperial consciousness to set the standards for human communities.

Who or what are some of the transnational corporations with so much power worldwide? That question is not easily answered because it depends on what is measured. In the early 2000s, the most capitalized companies on the stock market were traditional longstanding "blue-chip" companies like Exxon, General Electric, and AT&T. A decade later the top companies were mostly tech companies, like Microsoft and Apple. Each year *Forbes* magazine publishes a list of top corporations based on a composite score weighing revenues, profits, assets, and market value. In 2019, the *Forbes* top ten included five corporations from China, four from the US, and one from Netherlands (Royal Dutch Shell). Apple remained in the top ten, but the other big tech companies fell lower. Banks came out on top in 2019, including several from the US—JPMorgan Chase, Bank of America, and Wells Fargo—as well as a number of Chinese banks—ICBC, China Construction Bank, Agricultural Bank of China, the Bank of China, and the Ping An Insurance Group, which has diversified into technology and banking.[8]

Meanwhile, the top ten of the Fortune Global 500 shows Walmart at the top (best revenues) and includes several oil and gas companies, as well as two automobile manufacturers (from Germany and Japan). Cornel West lists corporations with "seductively strong cultural influence," such as McDonald's, Starbucks, Walmart, Coca Cola, hip-hop, and Hollywood.[9] And physicist, farmer, and activist Dr. Vandana Shiva is concerned about "the dominant industrialized and globalized food system, controlled by a handful of corporations," especially the five seed and chemical giants: Monsanto, Syngenta, Bayer, Dow, and DuPont.[10]

In order to have a better sense of multinational corporate behavior, let us look at one example, that of Walmart, which was extensively covered in a special series by the *Los Angeles Times* in November 2003. Although this report is more than a decade old, Walmart's overall approach to worldwide corporate control has no doubt intensified.

Walmart is clearly an American success story, starting in 1950 when Sam Walton opened a five-and-dime store in Bentonville, Arkansas, which remains the headquarters of the corporation. Sam's idea was to slash prices as much as he could and still make a profit. When he opened his first Walmart in 1962, he continued to pass his savings on to his customers, figuring he would make up the difference in volume. And he did. By the mid-1980s, Walton was number one on the *Forbes* list of richest Americans. One could argue that what Walmart does to cut costs is admirable. Certainly, many of us purchase goods at their stores at lower prices than we can get anywhere else. How do they do it?

Starting at home, Walton continued to drive an old pickup truck and emptied his own trash. He always flew coach and shared hotel rooms on business trips, a practice that continues today with Walmart managers. Walmart employees are forbidden to unionize (or even talk to a union rep), must work overtime without pay, and receive lower wages than comparable local employees. Truckers must unload their own cargo or pay

Walmart to do it. (When Walmart moved into the urbanized Los Angeles area, proposing to sell groceries as well as other items, grocery and teamster unions went on the longest strike in Southern California history. At that time, Walmart was paying its employees an average of $10 less an hour in wages and benefits than the existing local grocery stores.) When a Walmart store moves into town, competitors are often wiped out.

By the standards of the market culture, this is just good business. But it is not the way it used to be: when General Motors Corp brought prosperity to factory towns, a high-wage unionized worker could afford a house, a decent car, and maybe even a boat by the lake. But Walmart acknowledges that a full-time worker at one of their stores more recently might not even be able to support a family on a Walmart paycheck, while (in 2003) Walmart's CEO made nearly $18 million in salary, bonus, and stock.

In the beginning, Sam Walton was an avid "buy America" fan. But eventually the company realized that American producers were unable to meet their lowest price requirements, so Walmart made their way to Bangladesh and Honduras with their large populations of poor, young women willing to work from dawn to dusk for a few pennies an hour. Initially, Walmart asked for no more than cheap products, but gradually labor activists became aware that factories often lacked ventilation, fire escapes, and adequate bathroom facilities, and that a high percentage of laborers were merely children. As a large buyer, Walmart can and sometimes does intervene to make changes, but it often undermines such good efforts with its incessant push for lower prices. When Walmart demands faster production rates, employees may have to work eighteen-hour days for ten to fifteen days at a time to fill big orders. And, as when their US producers failed to meet production and cheap quotas, Walmart (and other transnational retailers) looks for ever faster and cheaper suppliers, which they are now finding in China with its low-cost raw materials and modern factories, highways, and ports. It does not take much imagination to see the implications for a local third world economy if a major buyer like Walmart decides to withdraw from its factories in one country. Is it still just good business practices?

In his column in the *Los Angeles Times* after the Walmart series was published, columnist Steve Lopez summarized the problems with this American practice:

> Because of the way Wal-Mart does business in America and beyond, (A) Your Uncle Ed's factory went under and he's on the dole; (B) A couple dozen merchants get rocked by the ripple effect; (C) A nail was driven into the coffin that used to be a quaint downtown; (D) That Honduran mom made $7 for 10 hours of toil; (E) A Chinese company is probably plotting to underbid the Hondurans; (F) Wal-Mart execs padded their mega-million-dollar portfolios; (G) And our taxes are going up because Wal-Mart employees who can't afford health insurance are dragging themselves into the county hospital emergency room. . . . And finally, that Honduran mom sews sleeves onto roughly 1200 shirts a day and there's no extra pay for extra work, but her bosses regularly remind her that she's lucky to have a job at all.[11]

That's the role in the global empire typically played by US-based transnational corporations. Obviously, there are exceptions. But when profit is God, a fella's gotta do what a fella's gotta do. If he doesn't, someone else will.

Pillar 3: Military Force

The three primary components of the US global empire work together. The first, an unfettered desire for more and more wealth gathered into fewer and fewer hands, is ensured by the extra-governmental World Bank and its companion institutions, the International Monetary Fund and the World Trade Organization. The second, the domain of transnational corporations, with its investments scattered all around the world yet funneling income back to its US stockholders, needs to be "secured." And therefore, the necessary third component is a vast and powerful US military force equally distributed around the world to ensure that there are no unexpected interruptions to this huge flow of money.

At the outset of this discussion of the role of the US military in the global empire, let's take a moment to notice how *odd* it is that safety and security are immediately associated with military force. Perhaps it is not odd to most of us because we are so accustomed to that equation in America. We not only equate security with military force, but we also typically equate peace with military force. We tend to believe that the only way to demonstrate strength is physically to overpower others. And yet strength can take many other forms than threat or force, and threat power is notoriously ineffective at bringing about peace. Thirty years ago, the Quaker economist Kenneth Boulding described at least three different faces of power: (1) *threat* power (do something I want or I'll do something you don't want), (2) *exchange* power (give me something I want and I'll give you something you want) and (3) *integrative* power (I'm going to do what I believe is right, and we will end up closer).[12] The reason we know so little about integrative power is because it is the purview of active nonviolence, practiced so effectively by Mahatma Gandhi and Dr. Martin Luther King Jr., but so unlike the power of threat that it is often invisible to us.

For now, let's consider the heavy reliance of our own American empire on military (threat) power. It was American political scientist Chalmers Johnson who definitively blew the whistle on the extent of our worldwide US military presence, in his books *Blowback* and *The Sorrows of Empire*.[13] Johnson reports:

> The United States dominates the world through its military power. . . . (with) a vast network of American military bases on every continent except Antarctica . . ., and well over half a million soldiers, spies, technicians, teachers,

> dependents, and civilian contractors in other nations and just under a dozen carrier task forces in all the oceans and seas of the world. . . .
>
> Our globe-girding military and intelligence installations bring profits to civilian industries, which design and manufacture weapons for the armed forces or undertake contract services to build and maintain our far-flung outposts. . . .
>
> As of September 2001, the Department of Defense acknowledged at least 725 American military bases existed outside the United States. Actually, there are many more.[14]

Johnson's book quoted here was published in 2004, and the American empire has intensified its military presence since then. Let's take a look.

US Military Bases. Johnson's basic argument holds, and this chapter looks more fully at America's worldwide military presence, although it is not easy to get accurate and current data. News media are not allowed on foreign military installations, except on rare occasions and for specific reasons. In order to save money but extend US military presence, a new generation of bases called "lily pads" (as in a frog jumping across a pond toward its prey) have been deployed in small, secretive, inaccessible facilities with a limited number of troops and weapons, but capable of mushrooming at need.[15] Although the Pentagon was required to close over 500 large and small bases in Iraq and is continuing to close bases in Germany and other areas, inquiries generally find that the United States probably maintains more than 1,000 military installations outside the 50 states, although this is not officially confirmed. A 2007 editorial in *The Christian Century* noted tongue-in-cheek that "even the Pentagon may not know how many military bases the US has overseas."[16]

US Military Budget. The primary federal department overseeing military spending is called the Department of Defense. It has long since been assigned many responsibilities that go far beyond the "defense" of the US except by the most generous interpretations of the word. Recall President Bush's 2003 speech at West Point, articulating a US policy of "preventive and unilateral" war, supporting his announced aims of extending the "blessings" of democratic capitalism to countries across the world. In principle, that policy has never been revoked, not by Democratic nor Republican administrations. Rather than a Department of Defense, in practice, we have a Department of Permanent War, with no plans in view to change that.

Depending upon whom you query, there are many answers to the question of the US budget for the military. No disagreement exists, however, about the fact that the US allocates more money to military spending than the combination of the next group of countries. With its 2020 budget of about $778 billion, the US spent "almost as much on its military as the next 12 largest spenders combined." Also in 2020, the International Institute for Strategic Studies reported that the US spent a significantly higher percentage of its gross domestic product on defense (3.7 percent) than any other country, accounting for approximately 39 percent of total global arms spending.[17]

The US budget for the military is not limited to the Department of Defense but is scattered throughout the entire federal budget, as well as in supplemental set-aside funds. At least ten separate pots of money are dedicated to fighting wars, preparing for wars, and cleanup after wars already fought. The fiscal year 2020 budget begins with the Pentagon's base budget for operating funds, preparing for ongoing "wars" never authorized by Congress, and high-priced weapons systems. It includes $9.6 billion in mandatory spending that goes toward military retirement and is publicly reported at a total of $544.5 billion. (In addition to this, President Trump proposed adding a future—nuclear equipped—Space Force at an estimated cost of $13 billion over the next five years.)

What does "high-priced weapons" mean? Two examples at the higher end will suffice. The Ford class aircraft carriers, produced by Huntington Ingalls Industries, have traditionally been used to showcase strength globally, but the latest model, costing $13.2 billion *per aircraft*, has a launch system that fails to launch and recover aircraft, and the ship's toilets clog frequently and can only be cleaned with specialized acids that cost about $400,000 a flush. A second example is Lockheed Martin's F-35 Joint Strike Fighter Lightning II airplane, now in its fifth generation, described by Lockheed as "an American family of single-seat, single-engine, all-weather stealth multirole combat aircraft." The F-35 has a price tag of $1.4 trillion over the lifetime of the program. But by 2014, it was $163 billion over budget and seven years behind schedule.

Continuing with 2020 budgeted items for the military, start with the base Pentagon budget of $544.5 billion. The Pentagon also maintains an Overseas Contingency Operations (OCO) account, which is billed separately to pay for the War on Terror, that is, our continuing military operations in Afghanistan, Iraq, Somalia, Syria, and elsewhere. That amount is added to the $554.5, for another $174 billion. This amount included $9.2 billion in "emergency" funding for President Trump's wall on the US-Mexico border.

The Department of Homeland Security, created in 2001, swallowed twenty-two existing government organizations, including, for example, ICE (Immigration, *or not*), FEMA (emergency management), the Secret Service, and other organizations, and proposes a budget of $69.2 billion. The State Department budget includes $51 billion for military aid efforts that we support in a dozen countries, including Israel and Egypt, and seventeen intelligence agencies also take another $80 billion. An item for "defense-related activities," in the amount of $9 billion, goes to the FBI for activities related to homeland security. The Department of Veterans Affairs gets another $216 billion for ongoing support to the almost three million veterans who remain in need of substantial care to deal with the physical and mental wounds of war.

Costs for all *nuclear* weapons are assigned to the Department of Energy, for new nuclear weapons and launching systems, research, maintenance, and cleanup, adding an additional amount of $24.8 billion to the current annual budget, but not including a proposed federal commitment to spend an additional $1 trillion over the next thirty years to "modernize" our nuclear arsenal.

Although it is sometimes excluded from military expenses, it is only fair to include in military costs the Pentagon's share of annual national debt total, which in 2020 was estimated at $156 billion. All these additional costs from federal departments other than defense bring the total of 2020 US military expenditures to $1.0979 trillion, according to *The Nation* magazine's research. That is to say, total annual military costs are roughly double the basic $544.5 billion officially set aside for defense.[18] Considering that the total proposed federal budget for 2020 was $4.8 trillion, the total means that one quarter of our annual federal budget is directly devoted to military purposes. In order to protest this distortion in values, the Milwaukee Advocacy Team of the Friends Committee on National Legislation joined World Beyond War and other organizations in 2020 to support a billboard reading "Three Percent of U.S. Military Spending Could End Starvation on Earth," with the support of their local congresswoman and county supervisor.

The General Accounting Office has been unable to render an opinion on consolidated financial statements even for the Defense Department itself, due to "serious financial management problems at the DOD that made its financial statements unauditable."[19]

Other Aspects of Militarization. By and large, members of both political parties in Congress support a high, sustained level of military spending. Near the end of his presidential term, Dwight Eisenhower used the now-familiar term, "military-industrial complex," and warned of the problems America would have if any of our future presidents lacked the knowledge he had gained of the interlocking strategies of governmental defense spending and the savvy of private military contractors. As Eisenhower anticipated, over the years, private military contractors have carefully arranged to have portions of the expensive military equipment they produce scattered within the boundaries of every state in the Union, thus ensuring that each congressional district holds many workers employed in the defense industry. Few elected officials are willing to risk losing local jobs caused by base closures in their states.[20] Congress is also reluctant to allow the Defense Department to cut other costs, like military health benefits and the growth of military pay. Some feel the cuts jeopardize national security. Not only that, but the congressional members of the House Armed Services committee are the top recipients of defense industry campaign contributions.[21]

There are so many competing agencies around the military in Washington, DC, surrounded by a universe of private intelligence contractors, all enswathed in secrecy, and they have grown so large that intelligence is now a ruling way of life in Washington—and it, too, has been thoroughly militarized. Even diplomacy is militarized, with diplomats working ever more closely with the military, while the State Department is transforming itself into an unofficial arm of the Pentagon. Militarization in the US is hardly new, but nowadays there seems to have been an accompanying transformation of the entire mindset of Washington—what might be called the militarization of solutions. More and more frequently, problems facing the country are framed in militarized terms, and the only possible solutions are considered from this mindset. One is reminded of the old saying, that "if one's only tool is a hammer, every problem looks like a nail."[22]

A few additional aspects of military expense require special mention. The Congressional Research Service document titled, "Conventional Arms Transfers to Developing Nations, 1999–2006," compared the value of military sales and military aid from wealthy governments to developing nations in 2006, noting that the value of the US share was $14 billion out of a world total of $27 billion.[23] Presumably we are not selling high quality armaments to countries with which we are presently at war, but it seems certain that eventually some of those weapons will be turned back against us, or at least such sales will contribute to ongoing micro-wars throughout the world. A second concern is the way we are disposing of our surplus military materials. Both the Department of Defense and the Department of Homeland Security have militarized more than 8,000 local domestic police forces and other domestic law enforcement agencies, to the tune of more than $7.4 billion, since they were authorized to do so in 2002. This means that weapons of war such as tear gas, tank-like armored vehicles, and high-powered guns are being used domestically against American citizens and especially communities of color.[24] The extent of such exchanges had become so severe that in early 2021, the House passed a bill (HR 1280) called the George Floyd Justice in Peace Act, which among other things will limit the Pentagon's transfer of combat-level equipment to state and local police.[25]

A third concern emerges from what is quite frankly a personal anecdote. Many years ago, my husband was employed as a physicist at Aberdeen Proving Ground in Maryland. One day he was sent to represent the agency at a meeting in the Pentagon. He reported that two of those present were arguing about the potency of a particular weapon. Finally, exasperated, one of them shouted: "You don't understand. Your device will only create 5.6 mega-corpses, whereas my device will create 6.7 mega-corpses!" My husband said he went home and resigned his position. The precise numbers are invented by me because I wasn't there, but the terminology is exactly as remembered.

Challenge to These Signs of the Times

Many citizens are not at all at ease with the enormity of US resources dedicated to killing people. Benedictine author and speaker Sister Joan Chittister writes in anguish to the Catholic bishops, "How can we possibly say that to abort a fetus is morally wrong but that the weapons intended only to abort the whole human race are not? . . . How is it that we can ask people to be prepared to die in nuclear warfare in the name of a 'defense' that is destructive but refuse to ask them to be prepared to die in passive resistance in the name of the gospel?"[26] Jim Wallis, American theologian, writer, teacher, and political activist, best known as the founder and editor of *Sojourners* magazine, argues that "support for US wars and foreign policy is still the area where American Christians are most 'conformed to the world' (Rom 12:2). This is our Achilles' heel, our biggest blind spot, our least questioned allegiance, the worst compromise of our Christian identity."[27] George Will, American libertarian-conservative political commentator and author, who writes regular columns for *The Washington Post* and provides commentary for *NBC News* and *MSNBC*, asks, "How can we forget, 27,394 days later, that U.S. bombs dropped on Hiroshima and Nagasaki, Japan (now considered to have 'small' nuclear payloads) killed between 150,000 and 226,000 people, often melting eyes in their sockets, and causing uncontrollable vomiting, diarrhea, bleeding gums, wounds that would not heal, disappearing white blood cells, fevers reaching 106 degrees . . . how can we forget the horrors caused by dropping nuclear bombs, much less plan to 'modernize' our arsenal to keep it up-to-date?"[28]

Cornel West challenges as one of the prevailing American dogmas of our time an aggressive militarism that takes the form of unilateral intervention, colonial invasion, and armed occupation abroad, "and posits military might as salvific in a world in which he who has the most and biggest weapons is the most moral and masculine, hence worthy of policing others." West continues that this closely held dogma "sacrifices U.S. soldiers, who are disproportionately working class and youth of color, in adventurous crusades . . . Domestically, this dogma expands police power, augments the prison-industrial complex, and legitimates unchecked male power (and violence) at home and in the workplace."[29]

Ruby Sales, an African-American social justice activist, scholar, and public theologian who works with youth in a fellowship program, says that she often asks them, "What does it mean to exist in a militarized state designed to protect the interests of a global elite and decimate our ability to resist and even think critically about the world that we live in? . . . How is it that you measure a person's worth? By their money, their proximity to celebrities, by the fact that this video went viral? Where is hope and meaning in a life of such insurmountable greed and social malformation?"[30]

Say it again, Ruby. Where is hope and meaning in a life of such insurmountable greed and social malformation? Can we answer her question?

Is this the world we want to live in?

Before closing this chapter, I want to say a brief word about the prophetic imagination. Recall that one of the chief aims of imperial consciousness is to paralyze the imagination. The world of the American global empire has for a long time asserted that our only real security is obtained by war, weapons, and violence, and very few of us these days feel confident to challenge that assertion. We actually seem to believe that violence brings peace, in spite of all the evidence to the contrary.

Violence dehumanizes and humiliates people, not only those who are beaten and killed, but *also* those doing the beating and killing. At least since the time of Jesus, it has been obvious that the way to peace is the way of love and generosity. In our later times, both Gandhiji and the Rev. Dr. Martin Luther King Jr. have dramatically revealed the amazing power and sustaining healing that can emerge from the way of active nonviolence. Both of them paid a great price (as did Jesus) so that we could hear this truth clearly and bear it proudly. Yet our own imperial consciousness assures that we American people remain largely blind to the only assured way to peace and loving community. Later, this book seeks to be explicit about the way love and generosity can be revealed to our imaginations as the gift of hope it is and brings. Let us pray that it be so.

Interlude B

Living in Hope

When we look clearly at the de-forming effects of market culture and global empire on our country, it may seem overwhelming. We might feel hopeless in the face of well-entrenched policies. On the other hand, if we do not look clearly at these patterns, we allow them to continue unchecked in our ignorance and denial. Small increments of the imperial market inevitably touch our daily lives, but when they become dominating patterns of US presence at home and abroad, we see the sharp contrast between what we are as a nation and the avowed moral commitments our founders set for us—to do good to all, to strengthen our souls, and to punish crime and reward virtue.[1]

So where, then, do we find hope? In the face of totalizing policies, how can we sustain hope for our lives and our country? Heartfelt hope is not securely birthed in optimism nor in a sense that things look good and are going well. If we want to bear the truth, we must first let suffering speak, and allow it to touch our hearts. We must be willing to spend some time in the darkness, blind at first until gradually seeing what is revealed there. "Night is all around us, even at noon, in the gloom of poverty, despair, fear, hunger. Night is also within each of us, in that secret place that is unreconciled, unhealed. But to dwell on and dwell in that darkness only makes us tired—and the night seems even longer. In the Scriptures, the chosen people understood this, . . . and refused to lose hope."[2] They knew they were not alone. Hope is a *decision* to which

God invites ancient Israel and contemporary America, a decision against despair, against oppression, barrenness, and indeed, even against suffering. Hope is grounded in God's promises and in God's call, as together we weep for what has been lost and together imagine what may yet be found.[3]

One of the strongest advocates of hope in recent years was that amazing man, Václav Havel, who was for many years an activist, outsider, and even prisoner in Communist-dominated Czechoslovakia. Yet he refused to dull and diminish his voice, eventually became president of the new Czechoslovakia after Communist rule. Hear what he said, while still on the "outside":

> Hope is a dimension of the soul, and it's not dependent on any particular observation of the world or estimate of the situation. It is an orientation of the spirit, an orientation of the heart; it transcends immediate experience and is anchored somewhere beyond its horizons . . . something we get, as it were, from "elsewhere." . . . The only real hope for people today is probably a renewal of our awareness that we are rooted in the earth and, at the same time, in the cosmos. This awareness endows us with the capacity for self-transcendence. Universal respect for human rights derives from respect for the miracle of Being, the miracle of the universe, the miracle of nature, the miracle of our own existence.[4]

In the Old Testament, the prophet Jeremiah, well-known for his laments during the time of the Hebrew exile in Babylon, nevertheless reports God as saying to the people, "For surely I know the plans I have for you, says the LORD, plans for your welfare and not for harm, to give you a future with hope. Then when you call upon me and come and pray to me, I will hear you. . . . I will let you find me" (Jer 29:11-14). And in the New Testament, we receive the assurances of St. Paul that the faith of Abraham, "the father of us all," was centered in belief in the God who "calls into existence the things that do not exist.

Hoping against hope, [Abraham] believed [in the promise of God] . . . being fully convinced that God was able to do what he had promised" (Rom 4:17-18a, 21). Both passages call us today to hoping against hope, beyond the ordinary yet within the present moment, believing in the promise of God however unlikely it may seem. And why? Because something strong within us is stirred, not to violence but to the persistent and often difficult way of love.

To go a little deeper into the mystery of hope, I turn to one of my favorite twentieth-century philosophers, the Frenchman Paul Ricoeur, whose biography is filled with paradoxes. A lifelong Christian, Ricoeur was nevertheless committed not to "play tricks" with philosophy (often called *Deus ex machina*, or having God "pop out" in the midst of a problem—as from a vending machine—in order to make things come out the way we want). As Ricoeur probed the depths of philosophy, he became increasingly interested in the "surplus of meaning" that can arise in a text, often resulting in new meanings emerging in language. By their multi-valence, metaphor, narrative, story, and myth potentially enable new meanings, new understandings, to emerge in language and life. In Ricoeur's own work, the term "possible worlds" begins to emerge. My hunch is that Ricoeur's use of this term was a legitimate way of opening philosophical concerns to the realm of the sacred. In the consideration of "possible worlds," we allow ourselves to be open to ideas we might previously have thought impossible. In a world dominated by imperial consciousness, we urgently need to find ways to break the walls set up to manage and contain our thoughts and ideas. Prophetic hope engages our imagination beyond totalism's walls. Recall Maimonides's statement quoted in chapter 1, that "prophetic hope is belief in the 'plausibility of the possible,' as opposed to the 'necessity of the probable.'"

As we continue seeking a clear vision of the de-forming patterns we experience today in America, let us not forget prophetic hope, which will bless and strengthen us, even in the face of what may seem to be overwhelming problems, because we trust in God's promises, believing God is able to do what has been promised. The blessing below is not an easy one, but with the spiritual practices described in section III of this book, we can learn to take joy in such a life.[5]

I have seen the blessing below described both as Franciscan and as Benedictine. Accepting that it is founded in practical wisdom, let us take time with it, as it helps us remember why and how to be people of hope:

- May God bless you with discomfort at easy answers, half-truths, and superficial relationships, so that you may live deep within your heart. Amen.

- May God bless you with anger at injustice, oppression, and exploitation of people, so that you may work for justice, freedom, and peace. Amen.

- May God bless you with tears to shed for those who suffer from pain, rejection, starvation, and war, so that you may reach out your hand to comfort them and to turn their pain into joy. Amen.

- May God bless you with enough foolishness to believe that you can make a difference in this world, so that you can do what others claim cannot be done. Amen.

CHAPTER FIVE

Denial of Earth's Climate Crisis

The fields are devastated,
the ground mourns;
for the grain is destroyed,
the wine dries up,
the oil fails. . . .
[T]he crops of the field are ruined.
The vine withers,
the fig tree droops.
Pomegranate, palm, and apple—
all the trees of the field are dried up;
surely, joy withers away
among the people. (Joel 1:10, 11b-12)

Planetary Beginnings

"This fragile earth, our island home"—this poetic language is one of my favorite descriptions of our planetary home.[1] For many years, however, it was believed that the earth was not at all fragile; indeed, we thought that "the natural state of the universe was one of infinite stability, with an unchanging earth anchoring the predictable revolutions of sun, moon, and stars."[2] So fixed was this notion in the human mind that, from Copernicus to the present day, "every scientific revolution that challenged this notion . . . was met with fierce resistance."[3] We want to believe that the earth is a stable, inert base providing unlimited resources, on which we humans can depend to satisfy all our desires.

Ever since Louis Agassiz's examination in 1837 of the geo-logic record, however, scientists have developed detailed knowledge of how Earth's climate has varied in the last few million years, as well as having fairly reliable scientific hunches going back to the beginnings of our 4.5 billion-year-old planet. Most of us are familiar with the concept that Earth has experienced periodic ice ages, interspersed with periods of glacial withdrawal. Perhaps fewer of us know that dramatic planetary climate changes have been caused "naturally" over these millions of years by such things as oscillations in Earth's orbit.

Let us remind ourselves of Earth's amazing planetary evolution. As presently understood in the scientific story of cosmogony, physicists envision a time of intense concentration of all matter-energy in a single unity, a single cosmic nucleus. Around eighteen billion years ago, this nucleus exploded, releasing intensely charged, radiant light-waves creating space and time as it expanded. Various forms of force were differentiated, such as gravity (to arrange the relation of the galaxies to the stars to the planets) and electromagnetic, nuclear, and sub-nuclear forces (to arrange atomic nuclei and atoms). As the first stars formed, burned, and exploded, additional basic atomic elements came into being, creating new stars and planets. Our planet, Earth, condensed about 4.5 billion years ago, some 13.4 billion years after the beginning of the universe. "All the atomic elements that make up earth, from rocks to the human body, are ultimately 'stardust.'"[4]

For the first billion years or more, Earth would have been inhospitable to the life that later evolved on its surface, for its atmosphere consisted mostly of water vapor, carbon dioxide, sulfur dioxide, chlorine, and nitrogen. Eventually complex organic molecules began to form and produce a primitive form of photosynthesis, the key to life on our planet. Multicelled bacteria evolved into aquatic animals and plants in the seas, gradually emerging on land. "It took about 3.9 billion years, some eight-ninths of earth's history, simply to generate photo-synthesizing bacteria. The entire evolution of land plants and animals has taken place in the last one-ninth of earth's history. Within that history of land animals, humans occupy a fraction of time, a mere 400,000 years."[5] It is important to note that the emergence of these primitive photosynthesizing bacteria did affect subsequent planetary life. As Kerry Emmanuel, atmospheric scientist at the Massachusetts Institute of Technology (MIT), observes, "Early life dramatically changed the planet. We humans are only the most recent species to do so."[6]

Climate Influences

Our sun is, of course, the primary natural source of light and heat for our planet. If the sun's ultraviolet radiation were transmitted directly to Earth, its intense ultraviolet strength would prove harmful to all life. But Earth's electromagnetic atmosphere, consisting of the layer closest to earth (the troposphere) and the separate layer closest to the sun (the stratosphere), occupies the distance between sun and earth, creating a sort of buffer. The stratospheric ozone layer absorbs radiation from the sun, protecting earthly life from the harshest UV radiation. Depletion of this layer of ozone leads to higher UV levels, and a number of ozone depleting substances (ODS) have been identified, including the familiar CFCs (chlorofluorocarbons). Ozone itself is a greenhouse gas, but its harmful effects depend on where it is located in the atmosphere; in the troposphere ozone only lasts for a short period.

The US Environmental Protection Agency describes the major sources of atmospheric pollution as increasing concentrations of carbon dioxide, methane, nitrous oxide, halogenated gases, and other manufactured greenhouse gases, all of which have risen significantly over the last few hundred years.[7] However, the basic effect of greenhouse gases on planetary temperature is complicated by other factors scientists continue to investigate, such as changes in the amount of water in the atmosphere, relative humidity, shifts in the tilt of Earth's axis with seasonal change, and the fundamental chaotic unpredictability of climate. But changes in climate also occur because of what scientists call "forced" variability, which could be something like volcanic activity.

Today human activity is the primary cause of forced climate change, to the extent that some observers are calling this the "Anthropocene" geological era. By comparing data on climate change before the industrial revolution of the nineteenth century and also simulating computer models (of vast complexity) about the climate in the twentieth century, scientists can make reasonable estimates of how the system varies naturally and then compare that with data from the last one hundred-plus years, demonstrating human-forced contributions to changes in Earth's atmosphere. The Massachusetts Institute of Technology and collaborators conducted two sets of computer simulations of the global average surface temperature throughout the twentieth century, the first applying only natural, time-varying forcings, and the second adding in the human-made forcings. Repeating this exercise with slightly different initial states and using many different climate models, a strong divergence begins to show up in the 1970s, and by the end of the twentieth century there is no overlap at all. In other words, the consistent results of MIT's study show a significant increase in global warming throughout the last third of the twentieth century, parallel to the heavy development of industrial production dependent on fossil fuels.[8]

Today it is clear that fossil fuels are the major contributors to forced and rapidly increasing climate warming, and that the industrial nations, including especially the US, are the primary polluters of the atmosphere, causing radical climate change. In 2016, the Paris Accords established a global goal of no more than two degrees Celsius of increased atmospheric warming, and set a global goal regarding climate of "enhancing adaptive capacity, strengthening resilience and reducing vulnerability to climate change, with a view to contributing to sustainable development and ensuring an adequate adaptation response in the context of the temperature goal."[9] By 2019 no single industrial nation was on track to meet the Paris goal, and President Trump had withdrawn the US from the agreement. (One of President Biden's first actions in 2021 was to restore American participation in the Paris Agreement.) By 2020, many countries had created significant ways to measure progress, but funding sources to undertake the necessary work remained woefully inadequate. By May 2021, the World Meteorological Organization (WMO) indicated a 40 percent chance that within five years, earth temperature would exceed the Paris goal, and that by 2025 the world would set another record for the hottest year. In particular, the WMO projected that Atlantic hurricanes would continue to increase in frequency and intensity, and the US Southwest desert drought would continue.[10]

Possibly we might consider that two more degrees of heat Celsius, or even more, would not be so bad. In most parts of the world, the range of daily temperature from mid-day to midnight would be at least five degrees Fahrenheit, so we might ask, what's the big deal? These projections are not about localized shifts in temperature, however, but a shift in the whole atmosphere of Earth, though of course actual temperatures will continue to vary from place to place. For the most part, the industrialized nations have chosen politically not even to discuss a warmer world atmosphere, much less take serious steps to mitigate it, despite a growing number of worldwide, nonprofit voices raised in concern. The 2021 Glasgow Cop26 meeting of world leaders added some further limitations on fossil fuels, although again there is question of whether nations will follow up on commitments, while China and India, major coal producers and users, refused to accept language calling for a phase-out of coal.[11] Possibly climate issues are hidden or ignored because of fear, or perhaps because of "technocratic faith, which is really market faith."[12] Here, however, we must seriously consider potential or even probable implications of the climate trajectory on which our world is presently engaged.

Climate Impacts

In 2020, David Wallace-Wells wrote a book focused not so much on the *science* of climate change, although he had spent many hours reading academic papers and in conversation with climate scientists, but rather, to describe *"the state of our collective understanding* of the many multiplying threats that a warming planet poses to all of us presently living on it."[13] Noting that in general scientists tend to be conservative in their public assessments of major hazards that Earth and all of its people might face, Wallace-Wells reports straightforwardly on the possible implications of continuing on our present worldwide course without major mitigation strategies. He urges us humans to look honestly at the possible effects on our human selves, because climate effects on nonhuman species have already been well-reported.[14]

One of the primary independent sources of scientific information on climate change is the United Nations group established in 1988, called the Intergovernmental Panel on Climate Change (IPCC). They currently offer a median prediction of over four degrees of warming (Celsius) by 2100 if we continue down the current emissions path, which would deliver astonishing impacts: hundreds of drowned cities while other metropolises across India and the Middle East would become so hot that humans could die merely by walking outdoors; wildfires in the American West and Australia would destroy many times the areas already smoldering; and "at four degrees, the deadly European heat wave of 2003, which killed as many as 2,000 people per day, will be a normal summer."[15] That said, it is almost impossible to predict upcoming weather precisely, because it depends on how quickly and fully mitigation measures are undertaken by many nations.

We cannot hope that climate will improve if current policies are not substantially changed. With that caveat, these are key elements of Wallace-Wells's projections, what he calls "Elements of Chaos."

Heat Death

Already "heat stress" is manifest worldwide—the five warmest summers in Europe since 1500 have all occurred since 2002.[16] Even if we meet the Paris limit of a 2 percent increase, cities like Karachi will annually have deadly heat waves like in 2015, when heat killed thousands in India.[17] In El Salvador's sugarcane region, one-fifth of the people who two decades ago were comfortably able to complete the harvest now suffer chronic kidney disease, the presumed result of dehydration while working the fields.[18] Cities are particularly at risk, since asphalt and concrete absorb ambient heat in daylight and release it after dark thus making it more difficult for human bodies to cool down at night, a process essential to health. "Currently, there are 354 major cities with average maximum summertime temperatures of 95 degrees Fahrenheit or higher."[19]

Drowning

A radical reduction in emissions to meet the two-degree goal could still produce a six-foot sea level rise by 2100. But "if we do not halt emissions, as much as 5 percent of the world's population will be flooded every single year."[20] "By 2100, possibly 2.4 million American properties, homes and businesses, farmlands and schools, or $1 trillion worth of our real estate could be underwater . . . And the sea level would continue to rise indefinitely."[21] Inland, global rainfall will continue to increase from the carbon already released into the atmosphere. Already, China is evacuating hundreds of thousands every summer to keep them out of the range of flooding in the Pearl River Delta.[22] As noted previously, any climate projection is uncertain, but sea level rise is somewhat different, because never before in human history have we experienced the breakup of ice at Earth's poles, so we don't know precisely how to judge the cascading sea effects. What we do know is that glacial ice does store greenhouse gases, such as methane and carbon, whose release into the atmosphere from melting glaciers will cause unknown but significant impacts.

Wildfires

The metropolitan area of Los Angeles, now with a population of over twelve million, has been built on what was originally barren desert. Perhaps we should not be surprised that it fluctuates annually between major fires and devastating floods, since it continues to try to support its growing population in such an arid area. But global warming has dramatically increased the danger there, causing severe fires to break out in the LA area in 1968, 1970, 1975, 1979, 1980, and 1982.[23] The most destructive wildfires in California history have hit the state since 2017.[24] In 2020, California experienced a twenty-year megaheat, and at least 6,500 square miles were burned by wildfire, doubling the previous record for area burned. Records continue to be broken, with five of the six largest wildfires in California history occurring in 2020. And wildfires are increasingly a global problem. For example, in 2018 in Sweden, forests *in the Arctic Circle* went up in flames, and in the same year, fire broke out in a Greek seaside resort, killing ninety-nine people.[25] Apart from the damage wildfires cause to human habitations, when forests burn, trees release their stored carbon. In previous climate periods, we could count on trees absorbing carbon and producing oxygen; now when forests burn, they release into the sensitive atmosphere all the amounts of carbon they have previously absorbed.

(Do take a breath here and return fully to your body before you read on. This is hard material to process.)

Dying Oceans

Ocean water covers 70 percent of Earth's surface and is the planet's predominant environment. More than a fourth of the carbon emitted by humans is sucked up by the oceans, resulting in "ocean acidification."[26] When carbon dioxide enters the ocean, it combines with seawater to produce carbonic acid, increasing the acidity of the water. A consequence of more acidic oceans is the binding of carbonate ions, which are used by marine creatures to make their calcium carbonate shells and skeletons. Acidic and warmer waters strip coral reefs of their fish food supply, which in turn means that the reefs can no longer support the marine life that in the past has provided food and income for roughly three billion people worldwide.[27] Further, as oxygen is crowded out of the seas by greater infusions of carbon, "oxygen-depleted dead zones" are created that cannot support marine life. "The number of such dead zones in our oceans has doubled each decade since the 1960s," causing mass extinctions of many fish populations, especially in the Gulf of Mexico and the coast of Namibia.[28]

Unbreathable Air

Higher concentrations of carbon dioxide produce many human health issues. For example, they cause cognitive ability to decline. Ironically, this effect is more noticeable in enclosed spaces, such as classrooms.[29] Air pollution has been linked with increased mental illness in children and the likelihood of dementia in adults.[30] Dust storms and ozone pollution increase as the planet warms, making the atmosphere dirtier, more oppressive, and more sickening. And already in 2012, the World Health Organization estimated *annual* global deaths from air pollution at about 7 million people.[31]

Food Production

Hunger and food production are near the top of the list of climate dangers, because for every degree of atmospheric warming, worldwide yields of staple cereal crops decline by 10 percent, although grain remains about 40 percent of the global human diet at present.[32] Such food losses will add other humans to the already 800 million people presently undernourished worldwide.

I have reserved the intertwined issues of climate, hunger, and food production for the last climate danger to be discussed here, because I chose to save those critical matters for the distinctive voice and important insights of physicist, farmer, and activist Dr. Vandana Shiva, primarily from her 2016 book, *Who (Really) Feeds the World: The Failures of Agribusiness and the Promise of Agroecology.* Shiva is an East Indian scholar who has been writing and acting on behalf of the environment for over thirty years. A member of the board of the International Forum on Globalization, she also is founder of Navdanya, a movement for saving seeds, protecting biodiversity, and spreading eco-logical methods of farming; she is not only a world-renowned physicist, but she also gets her hands into the soil.

Shiva begins by observing that "over the last ten thousand years, humanity has farmed ecologically. Systems and cycles of nature have given rise to renewal, reproduction, and diversity, allowing all beings to peacefully coexist, in sustainable systems that are in constant evolution."[33] In 1940, an English-man interested in colonization, Sir Albert Howard, wrote of India and China, "The agricultural practices of the Orient have passed the supreme test, they are almost as permanent as those of the primeval forest."[34] In other words, over the long history of human farming, a method had been developed that is genu-inely sustainable! However, the last fifty years have seen a disregard of that method as "primitive," with the substitution of "non-sustainable, chemical-intensive, water-intensive, and capital-intensive agriculture," which devastates natural envi-ronments and has resulted in widespread food insecurity.[35] The difference between the two approaches, Shiva says, is the difference between two knowledge paradigms. Traditional agriculture has its roots in the knowledge paradigm now called "agroecology," which takes into account the interconnected-ness of all life and nature's complex processes. In contrast, industrial agriculture emerges from a militarized way of think-ing that promotes violence toward the earth.[36] This is strong language, but Shiva means it as stated.

Food and agriculture today are sites for paradigm wars, each paradigm with its own type of knowledge, economics, and culture, each claiming to feed the world. Industrial agri-culture, the dominant paradigm today, "sees the world as a machine and nature as dead matter, at the heart of which is the Law of Exploitation." Shiva names this a militarized way of thinking that promotes violence because "it very literally uses the same chemicals that were once used to exterminate people now to destroy nature."[37] Here she is referring to the fact that after World War II, corporations that made explosives and chemicals for war, including for concentration camps, remodeled themselves as the agrochemical industry, using their synthetic and other chemical poisons in pesticides and herbicides.[38] This problem is also reported in Barbara Kingsolver's book *Animal, Vegetable, Miracle*, which reports that after World War II, "our munitions plants, challenged to beat their swords into plowshares, retooled to make ammonium nitrate surpluses into chemical fertilizers instead of explosives."[39] Agribusiness sees many insects and plants as enemies to be destroyed with poisons (which, after all, is what pesticides and herbicides do) made by their constantly improved technologies of violence. Operating out of the Law of Exploitation and Domination, transnational corporations use their procedures to "define what constitutes scientific knowledge, what an efficient food production system looks like, and what the boundaries of research and trade should be."[40]

Shiva's alternate paradigm is called the Law of Return, which retains continuity with time-honored ways of working together with nature. This law is "based on life and its interconnectedness, in which the human community acts as cocreators and coproducers with Mother Earth."[41] Biodiversity and water are managed as common, community shared resources. Plant waste becomes food for farm animals and soil organisms, and everything is recycled. Agroecology is based in small farms, often with women farmers who provide energy inputs through their own hard work and that of their animals, raise plants chiefly as food for family and neighbors, save seeds, and value diverse crops producing high nutrition. Globally, 70 percent of food that people eat comes from small-scale farmers working on small plots of land, but this fact is often hidden by calculations that look only at output, discounting energy inputs.[42] Shiva's colleague, Amory Lovins, boldly declares, "In terms of workforce, the population of the earth is not 4 billion but about 200 billion, the important point being that about 98 percent of them do not eat conventional food."[43] Shiva explains, "They don't eat food because *they are not people; they are energy slaves and they eat oil*. Industrial agriculture uses ten units of fossil fuel energy as an input to produce one unit of food as an output."[44] The leftover energy pollutes the planet. Indeed, *industrial agriculture is a massive contributor to climate change*, being "responsible for 25 percent of the world's carbon dioxide emissions, 60 percent of methane gas emissions, and 80 percent of nitrous oxide," all powerful greenhouse gases.[45] Some of those negative climate inputs are listed below, contrasted with ways to produce positive inputs.

Each of the chapters in Shiva's book calls out a particular ingredient in agroecology that contributes to healthy, abundant crops (and hence of food), in contrast to the claims of agribusiness. Let's look at some of the key ones, first in chart form I've prepared, then in text.

Who Really Feeds the World Chart

Agribusiness	Agroecology
Chemical Fertilizers	Living Soil
Toxic Monocultures	Biodiversity
Large-Scale Industrial Farms	Small-Scale Farmers
Seed Dictatorship	Seed Freedom

- *Living Soil Feeds the World, Not Chemical Fertilizers*. The soil is a living system, with billions of soil organisms creating, maintaining, and renewing soil fertility. Chemical fertilizers destroy healthy soils and have no water-holding capacity. Seeds and plants that have been chemically fertilized destroy healthy soil.[46]

- *Biodiversity Feeds the World, Not Toxic Monocultures.* More than seven thousand species have fed humanity through-out history, a remarkable indication of the biodiversity on our planet. But today, just thirty crops provide 90 per-cent of the calories in the human diet, and only three species—rice, wheat, and maize (corn)—account for more than 5 percent of our calorie intake. Industrial agriculture promotes monoculture, bred to respond to externally applied chemicals or toxins.[47] Long-distance trade means we generally produce not tomatoes but uniformly pretty rocks! The industrial emphasis on "yield per acre ignores the loss of nutrition that is leading to the malnutrition crisis."[48]

- *Small-Scale Farmers Feed the World, Not Large-Scale Indus-trial Farms.* Today just five corporations control the major-ity of seed, water, and land in the world and they are growing. The industrial giants controlling grain supply are Cargill, ADM (Archer Daniels Midland), Bunge, Glen-core International, and Louis Dreyfus.[49] US taxpayers actually subsidize large farm and seed corporations *and* their transport to far locations, at a rate Kingsolver esti-mates at about $725 per US household each year.[50] The theory that industrial agriculture produces greater output (with heavy fertilizer use), and thus can sell products more cheaply than small farms, is based on a confusing miscalculation of inputs and outputs. In a small farming system, outputs include the rejuvenation of soils, addi-tional food support for livestock and trees, diversity in outputs of crops that support each other's growth and nurture healthy human beings, "and the livelihoods created through cocreation and coproduction."[51] By dis-counting human involvement on a farm as a "job," and disregarding wastes and pollution, industrial production avoids mention of such "costs."[52] For global corporations, subsidies at home and artificially lowered values abroad translate into two-way profits. "For the farmer, they translate into a negative economy and increasing debts. Both at home in the US and in such far-off places as India, farmer suicides are spiraling."[53]

- *Seed Freedom Feeds the World, Not Seed Dictatorship*. For thousands of years, farmers, and especially women, have evolved and bred seed freely in partnership with each other and with nature. The seeds of small-scale farmers carry within them the knowledge of an agroecological, interconnected web of food and life. In contrast, in large-scale industrial farms, seed is patented by giant corporations, and laws prevent a seed from being used many times or being reproduced. Additionally, as we saw in an earlier chapter, the World Bank and its associates continue to strengthen a legal and economic framework for privatizing seeds and creating seed monopolies held by transnational corporations. The seeds developed over centuries by farmers are called "primitive cultivars" and *if* they are *even slightly* "modified by corporations to produce a generic seed form, they can be stolen, extracted and patented by large companies."[54] Furthermore, US and Canadian courts have ruled that if pollen from patented genes is transferred to another farm by insects or wind, up to a third of a mile, *the farmer must pay the corporation* for use of the (partially) patented seed.[55] Corporations are rupturing farmer-saved seed sources with HYVs (high-yielding varieties), hybrid seeds, and GMOs (genetically modified organisms). HYVs are high response varieties, heavily dependent on chemicals and fertilizers. Hybrid seeds are produced by crossing with genetically dissimilar species, and thus cannot be saved or replanted. And GMOs introduce genes from an unrelated organism into the cells of a plant.[56] Today, the top ten global seed companies control one-third of the annual $23 billion in commercial seed trade.

Many voices other than Shiva's have been raised against such practices of the large corporations, even in the United States. Why are we not listening? As Jesus says again and again, "You who have ears, listen!" Can we restore our people's strength to break through the blindness our big corporations and imperial consciousness have forced on us? Many years ago a small church group met with the CEO of a large corporation whose practices were killing people. One of the "housewives" in the group finally asked, "Can you tell your family what you are doing?" The CEO stood up and harshly said, "This meeting is ended." No wonder we live in a culture where often we would rather tell ourselves lies than face the truth of the cumulative impact of worshiping Money/Mammon. It is hard to face the truth that we use and abuse many others, especially if we must face it alone. Except that we are not alone; God assures us of that, and when we come together in God's name, we do find strength for the work of witness and challenge.

Concluding, Shiva notes that there *is* rising opposition to the food system under the Law of Exploitation: From 2007 to 2016, there were over fifty-one food riots in thirty-seven countries. Meanwhile, 40 percent of all greenhouse gas emissions responsible for climate change come from a fossil-fuel-based global system of agriculture.[57] In the US alone, we consume "about 400 gallons of oil per year per citizen—about 17 percent of our nation's energy use—for agriculture, a close second to our vehicular use."[58] The food system perpetuated by transnational corporations is badly broken on every measure that counts: sustainability, justice, and peace.[59]

Challenge to These Signs of the Times

This section has two parts: first, an important observation about the creation of energy from the Worldwatch Institute's 2015 *State of the World* report, and second, a more reflective section about what might be preventing a more vigorous response to the climate crisis, which in turn reveals a possible way forward.

Energy Creation

The 2015 Worldwatch report begins with a careful assessment of a major threat to sustainability that is not included in the list of causes and impacts above, but which may offer a basis for significant change because it has direct implications for our market culture, and hence may carry more leverage than mere appeals for cooperation. It is called the energy, growth, and credit nexus.[60]

Endless economic growth driven by unbridled consumption is foundational to modern economies. Yet we are on a collision course with planetary limits, as demonstrated above. Over the years, technological advances have enabled us to extract and utilize Earth's resources with few constraints, while we were creating a highly specialized fossil-fuel-based civilization that turns out to be inherently ecologically disruptive. Consider that world coal extraction increased 10-fold from 1900 to 2015, and world oil production, only begun in the late nineteenth century, increased 270-fold from 1900 to 2015.[61]

When we look for the foundation of our ability to create good profits, high salaries for those at the top, and at the same time, relatively inexpensive goods and services, we see all that is possible largely because of low-cost fossil energy.[62] Applying large amounts of fossil energy in order to mechanize tasks that humans once performed manually may have seemed like magic at first, but there is a direct relationship between cheap energy input and relatively inexpensive goods. "It takes energy to get energy," and we have already tapped the fossil energy stores that are easily accessible, so now "we need to *use* an increasing share of the energy we produce *in order to generate the energy*" we will need for the future.[63] When hard-to-access remaining energy supplies require increasing amounts of energy to harvest them, our society will have less surplus energy to expend on other things. It requires energy to build roads and hospitals, create iPhones, and support symphony orchestras. We can already see the dilemma, in the fact that real salaries are decreasing while health care and education are more expensive.

"Money is essentially a claim on a certain amount of energy. There are four kinds of real capital: natural (oil, trees, rivers), built (houses, tractors, computers), social (relationships, networks), and human (health, skills, knowledge)."[64] In the early 1900s, America had what seemed infinite wealth in natural resources, and banks began to create rules to lend money to match productive output. Essentially banks created money credit (debt) based on the availability of other forms of capital (rich natural resources, creative ideas, etc.). Cash is a claim on energy resources, while debt is a claim on *future* energy resources. From 2008 to 2016, "the Group of Seven nations (Canada, France, Germany, Italy, Japan, the United Kingdom, and the United States) have added about $1 trillion per year in nominal GDP, but only by increasing debt by $18 trillion-plus"—all in order to keep consumption high and GDP slowly growing.[65] Debt is increasing, while energy—both present and future—is declining.

In time, the higher costs of extracting fossil fuels will likely lead to the collapse of highly energy-intensive industries and practices, and everyone will experience the impact of widening and deepening poverty in a world where everything will be very expensive.[66] This is basic economics, but few of us have looked at climate change issues from this perspective. Future planning requires a low-carbon approach to energy usage, and a lower-consumption society. The way of life we have sustained in the US is *already beyond our means*. But the Worldwatch Institute reminds us that we of humanity are creative, flexible, and surprising, and those qualities are major resources in the case of needed change.[67]

We have been warned about a climate crisis for well over thirty years, but despite such paper responses as the Paris Accord in 2016, very little has been done at the governmental level to reduce deadly emissions into Earth's atmosphere. While most countries, including our own, have put off meaningful action, those least responsible for climate change are those most affected: poverty is woven throughout this whole climate story. Not only have we been verbally warned, we have actually seen the dramatic damage inflicted by global warming in the examples given earlier in this chapter. Still we resist taking up a vigorous governmental response, and this has been true of both political parties in the US. Multiple earthly species have died and parts of Earth are unlivable, yet still we hesitate. Robert Jay Lifton has invented the phrase "our national reality disorder," to describe our distrust of scientific facts, our denial of the rapidly accelerating climate disaster, and the "fake news" accusations, aided and abetted by rampant conspiracy theories.[68]

A possible explanation for such a national reality disorder might rest in the fact that in some respects we have been misled, both by the generic Christian world picture and the insistence of science on a split between fact and value. My experience is that thoughtful people both in Christianity and in science have in many cases shifted beyond previous biases that were narrow and even thought to be incontestable, but it is important to acknowledge that such biases existed and too often still govern general perceptions. David Korten, cofounder and board chair of the Positive Futures Network, calls the situation of two viewpoints coloring our reality "the problem of the Strict Father versus the Aging Clock."[69] "Strict Father" is an image of the Christian God as a distant male authority figure to whom humans owe unquestioning loyalty, a monarch in whose image humans are "the centerpiece of creation and the realization of its purpose."[70] In contrast, the "Aging Clock" emerges as an interpretation of Newtonian science proposing that the cosmos is composed of more or less inert matter that is running down to an entropic death, a machine completely, empirically verifiable, with no relationship to spiritual vagueness and ambiguity.[71] Neither of these images is really current, but both give us an image accounting for confused and uncertain minds that need to be introduced to new ways of thinking about climate change.

Cultural historian Thomas Berry picks up these themes by suggesting that our recent past has been an "effort to achieve human well-being in a consumer society by subduing the

spontaneities of the natural world with human manipulation
. . . (As a result), we find ourselves ethically destitute just
when, for the first time, we are faced with ultimacy, the ir-
reversible closing down of the Earth's functioning in its major
life systems."[72]

Let's take a moment here to allow ourselves to integrate
what we have just read. Unless we make major changes
quickly, our whole planet is likely to shut down. Have we
really allowed ourselves to believe that, among all the warn-
ings about climate change? Recall where this chapter began,
with the reminder that it has been human to believe the universe and our planet Earth are our primary source of stability.
How can our minds and hearts even begin to wrap themselves
around the idea that our one sure source of stability, Earth itself, is disintegrating—and of course, ourselves with it?!

Ecofeminist theologian Rosemary Ruether has a different
starting point, proposing "a vision of a source of life that is
'yet more' than what presently exists. . . . To believe in divine
being means to believe that those qualities (of caring) in ourselves are rooted in and respond to the life power from which
the universe itself arises."[73] She considers ecological healing
from "a theological and psychic-spiritual process," part of an
ecological ethics that, on the one hand, views the "entire planet
as a living system, behaving as a unified organism," which she
calls *Gaia* (the name of the Greek earth goddess), thus rooting
"human life in a source deeper than the merely biological."[74]
For nature's own ecological system is rooted in the "interrela-
tion of all things."[75] Such a view emphasizes the profound
kinship between humans and all other living things. This is
not merely suggesting a new name for the same old things; it
expresses a fresh viewpoint in which humans are not the masters and movers of creation but one of its members, mutually
committed to take and receive care.

Ruether is fully aware of the serious danger to our planet,
but she also gives us a new way of thinking about climate and
Earth. Her vision offers us an approach not only for prophetic

imagining but also a way to work together to nurture the repair and new unfolding of a healthy Earth. We dare not assume that this task belongs exclusively to those in political and economic leadership, because—as we know from the hundreds of polls conducted daily—our leaders are influenced by "what people think." But we can join together in various community groups toward a vision of Spirit and science together, recovering awe and wonder about the miraculous universe we share. At the base of this vision is a renewed sense of the sacred both in ourselves and in the precious Earth that has and will sustain us, when we affirm and act in accordance with our kinship.

Let us close with an excerpt from Teilhard de Chardin's "Hymn to the Universe":[76]

> Blessed be you, mighty matter, irresistible march of evolution, reality ever new-born: you who, by constantly shattering our mental categories, force us to go ever further and further in our pursuit of the truth.
>
> Blessed be you, universal matter, immeasurable time, boundless ether, triple abyss of stars and atoms and generations: you who by overflowing and dissolving our narrow standards or measurements reveal to us the dimensions of God.
>
> Blessed be you, mortal matter: you who one day will undergo the process of dissolution within us and will thereby take us forcibly into the very heart of that which exists.
>
> It is you, matter, that I bless.

CHAPTER SIX

Resistance to Diversity

[A] lawyer stood up to test Jesus. "Teacher," he said, "what must I do to inherit eternal life?" . . .

[W]anting to justify himself, he asked Jesus, "And who is my neighbor?" Jesus replied, "A man was going down from Jerusalem to Jericho, and fell into the hands of robbers, who stripped, beat him, and went away, leaving him half dead. . . . [A] priest . . . likewise a Levite, . . . passed by on the other side. But a Samaritan while traveling came near him; and . . . was moved with pity. He went to him and bandaged his wounds, having poured oil and wine on them. Then he put him on his own animal, brought him to an inn, and took care of him. The next day he took out two denarii, gave them to the innkeeper, and said, 'Take care of him; and when I come back, I will repay you whatever more you spend.' Which of these three, do you think, was a neighbor to the man who fell into the hands of robbers?" [The lawyer] said, "The one who showed him mercy."¹ Jesus said to him, "Go and do likewise." (Luke 10:25, 29-37)

Preliminary Thoughts: Biodiversity

Throughout this book, the notion of biodiversity arises often. Vandana Shiva has been particularly helpful in pointing out that sustainable agriculture does not happen under what she calls the Law of Exploitation. The life-giving alternative she advocates, the Law of Return, involves the mutually reinforcing qualities of healthy soil, seed freedom, local wisdom, natural pollinators, and plant diversity, all of which in turn rests in "life's interconnectedness, in which the human community acts as cocreators and coproducers with Mother Earth."[2] Somehow overall health in any earth community prospers better when diversity is present, when there is mutual regard for the unique "voice" or "valence" of each distinct ingredient, and all things work in harmony. Yet we often resist this truth when it comes to human community.

Wendell Berry speaks of the land he loves, "in the northern corner of Henry County, Kentucky."[3] Within that corner are many varied landscapes, each of which requires a particular type of care, often discovered by local farmers after years of experimentation and attentiveness to results. Berry advocates a system of decentralized, small-scale industries to transform the products of our fields and woodlands and streams. He realizes that he will be accused of being unrealistic. Yet, insisting that he wishes to be practical, he asks, realistic *according to whom*? "I am thinking as I believe we must think if we wish to discuss the *best* uses of people, place, and things, and if we wish to give affection some standing in our thoughts."[4] Ultimately, Berry points out "the inescapable final step in an argument for diversity: that without a diversity of people, we cannot maintain a diversity of anything else."[5]

Rosemary Ruether observes that healing, in people, society, and the physical environment involves both theology and a psychic-spiritual process. She sees that "a healed relation to the earth cannot come about simply through technological fixes [but] *demands a social reordering* to bring about just and loving interrelationship between men and women, between races and nations, between groups presently stratified into social classes," in contrast to contemporary life with its great disparities of access to the means of life.[6] Ruether urges that we need a vision of a source of life that is "yet more" than what presently exists. "Consciousness and altruistic care are qualities . . . often too poorly developed in our own species. To believe in divine being means to believe that those qualities in ourselves are rooted in and respond to the life power from which the universe itself arises."[7] In other words, the Mystery that is God is best understood as expressing itself in the sacred spark found in every corner of the universe, and most especially where cultural homogeneity is enriched and strengthened by the heterogeneity of fruitful diversity.

It seems to me that any affirmation of the value of diversity must also eventually come to the conclusion that healthy biodiversity must ultimately be diversity not only of plants and animals, but also of people. Our times are increasingly demanding a wide range of viewpoints speaking with equally powerful voices all gathered to participate at the same "table" where decisions are being made. Without biodiversity as an essential component of healthy agriculture, ecosystems lose resilience, efficiency, and stability.[8] I would argue that similarly, without human diversity, human societies also lose resilience, efficiency, and stability. No wonder we have so much division in contemporary American society, since we have for so long endeavored to eliminate or sideline legitimate and essential voices of Native peoples, Black and Brown peoples, Asian and Pacific Islander peoples. Rather than seek to be a "melting pot," let us aim for an authentic American community of beautiful mosaic pieces!

This perhaps overlong introduction to concepts of diversity reveals the similarity between ecological concerns and human diversity, and offers important insights to us about the considerable benefits diversity can and does produce in all Earth systems. The question posed by this introduction is this: If diversity is both essential and beneficial for robust plant and animal life, why do we so vigorously hold our White human culture apart from any other races, much less imagine it to be singularly superior? If healthy plants and animals depend on diversity, what makes us think that human beings can be healthy without rich diversity? It becomes obvious that the reason is to maintain "threat power," rather than welcoming the gutsy, life-giving integrative power.[9]

American Self-Image

At the port of New York harbor stands the mighty Statue of Liberty, proudly proclaiming, "Give me your tired, your poor, your huddled masses yearning to breathe free!" Although the statue was actually a gift from France to the United States as a sign of enlightenment, its colossal stance, coupled with Emma Lazarus's poem later mounted to its base, has caused it to be a powerful symbol of American idealism. The statue has symbolized our best self-image as Americans dedicated to freedom and opportunity for all, God-blessed because of the finer qualities we embody and seek to share. Abroad, the out-sized statue has long been a symbol of hope to generations of immigrants, although it must be said that White, European immigrants have received preference. In general, we (White) Americans like to think of ourselves as generous and welcoming, benign in our relationships with other peoples. No doubt this partly stems from our early conviction that, like the Israelites, we were God's chosen people, because we believed our democracy represented all that was good and superior in humanity.

The American historical record, however, clearly shows our consistent resistance to real diversity. From the beginning we displaced the proud "first peoples" who lived here, the Native Americans, who we forcefully moved off their lands and exterminated—all told, about ten million of them.[10] An article by an Episcopal bishop and Choctaw elder, the Rt. Rev. Stephen Charleston (who I much admire), begins by noting that when his father was born, he was not an American citizen because Native Americans were not citizens of this country until 1924, although they had lived on this land for thousands of years. Charleston goes on to say that community leadership among his people carried a strong emphasis on the ethical and spiritual, out of a conviction that no human system can endure unless it is built on truth. Further, he writes that the Choctaw insistence on truth "is not a stereotype of the noble savage perpetuated by Western colonialism. It's a warning flag from a civilization that witnessed firsthand the cost of lies":

> The promises made to us were lies. The stories told about us were lies. The motives for taking our land were lies. The reasons for destroying our culture were lies . . . (W)e know for certain: systems that do not depend on the truth become corrupt, self-destructive, and eventually lethal. . . . Over time, permission to lie consumes hope in a darkness that cannot be penetrated by any light of truth.[11]

American history continues with the institution of slavery, which in addition to many other evils, probably involved the deaths of another ten million people.[12] Hundreds and thousands of Africans, mostly enslaved, provided an essential workforce for colonies in the Americas and the New World. Beginning in 1619, the privateer ship, *The White Lion*, brought twenty African slaves ashore in the then-British colony of Jamestown, Virginia. Throughout the seventeenth and eighteenth centuries, people were kidnapped from the continent of Africa, transported by ship in horrendous conditions, forced into slavery in the American colonies, and exploited to work. They were considered possessions just like property, to be handled, bought, and sold at whim by plantation owners. By the 1860s, at the start of the Civil War, approximately four million enslaved people lived in the United States.

American history later continues with the US invasions of Guatemala, El Salvador, Chile, Brazil, and Venezuela, and the so-called Spanish-American War of 1898-1902, in which America took control of Cuba, Puerto Rico, the Philippines, Hawaii, and Guam. Gradually America overthrew constitutional governments especially in this hemisphere, installing right-wing leaders who would not challenge US policies. America's plan was not to follow Britain's model of trying to *govern* the world; instead, as Unitarian minister and then well-known columnist and editor Denny Ludwell reported, perhaps tongue-in-cheek, "we shall merely *own* it (the world)."[13]

What is at the root of these terrible events? We humans have told ourselves many stories that inform and sustain habits of mind, and one of the main ones is that any stranger is always a potential enemy. That notion is woven into many White people's sense of human history—the people from across the river, or from another country, or in any way different from us—all of them are potentially dangerous, and our first impulse is to treat them as an enemy or to try to expel them from the body politic in one way or another. Let's admit that initially, we can never know whether or not strangers will be enemies; indeed, that is a odd concept and not a very biblical one.

In the twentieth century, philosophers and scholars began to look seriously at the notion of "the other," perhaps because in the current global community, those who represent otherness may in fact be neighbors rather than strangers. Also, it has not escaped religious notice that Godself is truly the Ultimate Other! Therefore, it behooves us to learn to engage *any* other as sacred, to practice respect and regard, even awe, at the mystery of what is "not us," in order to develop qualities helpful to us in communing more fully with the One at the heart of the world.

We learn from the astonishing tale in early Scripture of the three "strangers" who visited the patriarch Abraham by the oaks of Mamre, when he and his wife were old and had not been able to have children (though he had had a child with his wife's Egyptian slave, Hagar—which is another story, and probably one filled with racism). Realizing that their guests were somehow important (sent by God?!), Abraham and Sarah fed the visitors a special meal. Then the "strangers" promised that Sarah would have a child, which did indeed come to pass (Gen 18). These strangers brought a blessing so great that it changed the history of Jews, Christians, and maybe Muslims too! In the fifteenth century, the Russian artist Andrei Rublev painted an icon of those visiting strangers, called *The Trinity*. It is a remarkable work, filled with grace and beauty, another symbol of the power of others to be unexpected and wonderful gifts.

To summarize the issues of biodiversity among humans, the following chart integrates some insights of Shiva's with portions of this discussion, as they overlap.

Monocultures of the Mind	Biodiversity in All Nature
Strangers threaten Stability	Strangers Offer Creative Possibilities
Fixed Order makes for Comfort	Apparent Chaos Resolves in New Creation
Big Sticks ensure Big Power	Compassionate Action offers Hope for New Possibilities

Structural Racism

The particular point to be emphasized here is that it is naïve to believe that the US policies described in this book were color-blind. From the very beginning, White supremacy is woven into the American story. Although democracy envisions "ordinary people living lives of decency and dignity, owing to their participation in the basic decision-making in the fundamental institutions that affect their life chances," this precious notion is difficult to create and sustain, given unformed human nature and especially given structural racism in America.[14] Indeed, it has been observed that, "without the presence of Black people in America, European-Americans would not be 'White,'—they would be Irish, Italians, Poles, Welsh—engaged in class, ethnic, and gender struggles over resources and identity. What made America distinctly American for them was not simply new opportunities and struggles, but Black slavery and racial caste as the floor upon which other issues could be diffused and diverted."[15] The latest federal action in this sorry story of unashamed racism is the 2016-8 attempt to build a high wall between the US and Mexico.

In fact, the very term "White supremacy" is a lie. No matter the position White Americans hold in our society, they/we cannot in truth claim to be superior to non-Whites. Yet the very structure of American culture shouts of the supremacy of White skin in business, politics, medical care, housing, education, and more. Racism has been embedded here for so long that even some well-intentioned White people claim to be unable to see structural racism. One simple example that appeared in the September 23, 2020, issue of *Christian Century* magazine reporting the results of a June 2020 American Values Survey shows that 81 percent of White Republicans and 72 percent of White evangelical Protestants say that "recent police killings of unarmed Black men are (not signs of racism, but) isolated incidents."[16] Yet recently in my community, police *killed* an eighteen-year-old young Black man with no prior history of arrest, for only speeding in the middle of the night on an interstate highway.[17] Today in America, roughly 40 percent of Black children live in poverty and almost 10 percent of all Black young adult men are in prison, often on the basis of a nonviolent drug offense.[18]

In 2020 and 2021, a scholarly concept called Critical Race Theory (CRT) spilled over into public conversation. CRT is actually an American academic concept more than forty years old, exploring the intersection between race and US law. The core idea is that race is a social construct, and that racism is not merely the product of individual bias or prejudice, but also something embedded in legal systems and policies. A good example is when, in the 1930s, government officials literally drew lines around areas deemed poor financial risks, often explicitly due to the racial composition of inhabitants. Banks subsequently refused to offer mortgages to Black people in those areas. Today, those same patterns of discrimination live on through "race-blind" policies, like single-family zoning that prevents the building of affordable housing in advantaged, majority-White neighborhoods, which thus stymies racial desegregation efforts. CRT has become something of a punching bag today, as some Americans feel highly threatened when they are asked to look at our history and present practices in the face, and some seem deliberately to misunderstand the basic concept. As a result, in early 2021, twenty-seven states had introduced bills or taken other steps that would restrict teaching CRT or limit how teachers can discuss racism and sexism. Twelve states have enacted these bans, either through legislation or other avenues.[19]

A further example of White Americans denying that structural racism exists in the US is the dismaying winter 2020 decision of seminary presidents in the Southern Baptist Convention that the Baptist Faith and Message was incompatible with Critical Race Theory. Jim Wallis, known for his advocacy on issues of peace and social justice, reflected on that statement and observed that these seminary presidents refused to face the theology at the core of what he called the original sin of our country—the lie, the myth, the ideology, and the idolatry of White superiority—in which God's children of color are at risk every day. Wallis adds his own conviction: "It is time to call upon our seminaries and our churches to begin the long spiritual process of discipling white American Christians out of the idolatry of racism—both personal and systematic."[20]

Many ways exist to examine White Americans' fear of and resistance to diversity. Especially since the killing of George Floyd, racism against Black Americans is near the top of the contemporary political agenda. Hence, the rest of this chapter will focus on that troubling fact of our polity. Political scientists routinely say that public policy is the authoritative allocation of value, and it is essential in our times to acknowledge that such political statistics result from deliberate policy decisions; they are not isolated incidents. Today, almost every social construct in America reveals the most vulnerable people to be Blacks, especially Black women.[21] Almost 140 million Black citizens are poor, or are just one fire, health crisis, job loss, or severe storm away from deep poverty; more than 12 million people have lost their employer-based health care, adding to the 87 million who already had inadequate health care; nearly 12 million renters are behind in rent and could face eviction in the coming months; and 26 million people reported not having enough to eat, while 72 million pounds of food goes to waste each year.[22] These statistics, too, are the result of deliberate policy decisions.

The Racial Script

Dr. Reggie Williams, professor of Christian ethics at McCormick Theological Seminary, offers a clear-eyed description of structural racism in his essay, "The Racial Script," in *Christian Century*.[23] Williams first notes that none of us can be unaware that Black people bleed and die, but we Whites may not realize just how prevalent and persistent White supremacy is in this country, remaining trapped within a history we do not understand but must act to change. He acknowledges that to act in response to America's racist history may be terrifying, requiring as it does a complete recalibration of White identity. He urges that we understand the recent police killings of George Floyd, Trayvon Martin, Ahmaud Arbery, and Breonna Taylor not as isolated incidents, but events within a premise that merges them all. "That premise is White supremacy, deeply embedded within the story this nation believes itself to be living."[24] After centuries of such reality-bending cruelty, we Whites owe it to ourselves to recognize what it is.

First, it is not about feelings, not a matter of liking or disliking people of different races.

It is also not about having contempt for people based on inaccurate information. Even unfounded bias or prejudice is insufficient to describe White supremacy. Williams describes White supremacy as "the manufacture and maintenance of systems and structures . . . populated by a fetishized, White ideal," a longing for an idealized community *exactly like me*.[25] This longing carries with it a script that is largely unconscious, yet it informs the common understanding of human difference and social interaction. All of us learn, from many teachers, from the day of our birth, that we are protagonists or antagonists in the story, not by choice or decision, but because that's the way it is. This script is not really entertaining and it has no grounding in reality, other than the alternate reality it has created, but its plotline always results in Black death.[26]

The plight of the antagonist, always White, follows a pattern in which there first is a blatant killing of an unarmed Black person, always a disproportionate response to a baseless fear. The killer's defenders inevitably discover some form of disparaging information about the character or behavior of the deceased, which is used to justify the killer and implicate the dead. "The Black victim is subsequently tried in the court of public opinion, using the evidence of a racial script as evidence against them in their own killing. . . . Somehow the Black dead deserved to die. In effect, the reality-bending nature of racism makes it logical to blame the dead for their own killing."[27]

Williams's story, this script, might seem highly improbable were it not for the fact that it very accurately describes the events of the killings of the four Black persons mentioned above, Floyd, Marten, Arbury, and Taylor, all in the last six months of this writing. And a Rutgers University study in 2013–2017 designed to quantify risk to American lives revealed that Black men, by far the most at-risk group, face 1 in 1,000 odds of being killed by the police over the course of their lives![28]

If Williams's script of racism were not horrible enough, scientific theorists in the eighteenth century provided taxonomies to "prove" that racial discrimination was justified. In 1735, Carl Linnaeus provided a taxonomy of *Europeanus* with blue eyes and an "inventive mind," governed not by caprice but by natural laws. Later, in 1752, Johann Friedrich Blumenbach added a few other traits making *Europeanus* beautiful, White, and Caucasian.[29] Once slave trading began from Africa, *Europeanus* found its perfect foil in the Negro. By 1790, the term "White" was a legal term applied to European colonists, synonymous with free citizen. By the time of the writing of the American Constitution, the Black slave was counted as only three-fifths of a citizen, "a product essential to the production of sugar cane, tobacco, and cotton."[30]

Williams's description of this racial theory adds that it required inventing character scripts for the "contented slave" (a Black under the complete authority of White people), the "comic Negro" (a blackface trying to be civilized and it's funny), and the "tragic mulatto" (race-mixing creates a pitiful creature), all of which are intended to suggest the vast distance between White and Black people in their capacities for civilized, intellectual, and moral living. "In preserving this template, White supremacy disfigures all embodied life. . . . To reveal this reality as it is will require the right tools—and courage."[31] Hear again the phrase: "disfigures all embodied life."

I ask the reader to stop now for a moment and try to breathe in that reality, and feel what you are feeling.

Again and again, from a variety of sources, most of us Whites have heard stories like the above script, yet very little changes. These dreadful things continue to exist, forming the foundations of structural racism, because at some level, those who make and support existing public policies at best don't care. Audre Lorde, an American writer self-described as "black, lesbian, mother, warrior, poet," puts the rationale succinctly:

> Institutionalized rejection of *difference* is an absolute necessity in a profit economy which needs outsiders as surplus people. As members of such an economy, we have *all* been programmed to respond to the human differences between us with fear and loathing and to handle that difference in one of three ways: ignore it; and if that is not possible, copy it if we think it is dominant, or destroy it if we think it is subordinate. But we have no patterns for relating across our human differences as equals.[32]

From Numbers to Real People

We who write to communicate with groups of people are told to offer specific data to support our positions. Yet as a woman, I find my heart and intention more often engaged from personal stories, from true anecdotes about real people. So, what follows next here is a story, created from many individual reports from real people I myself have known. Even as I do this, I acknowledge my inadequacy as a White person to really understand the full experience of racism.

The story begins . . .

My name is Ceraline Jefferson. One of my ancestors worked at then-President Jefferson's Monticello plantation, and since no slave was allowed to have a "surname" (my grandparents were not allowed to keep the name of our tribal community in Africa), here we were all called by our owner's name, "Jefferson." Today I am a forty-year-old Black woman, married, with three children, ranging in age from four to seven to twelve years old. My husband, Josiah, had a good job in a meat factory, but a couple of months ago, he got a severe case of the flu and had to miss three days of work. The company fired him the first day he didn't show up and gave his job to someone else before he was well. How could we have savings, living from paycheck to paycheck?! My husband immediately started looking for a new job and filed for unemployment payments. But there are not many decent jobs available, and as soon as they see a dark skin, their eyes pass right over you to the White man in line behind you. Before that, I had earned money each week as a seamstress, working at a couple of retirement homes a day a week. But my income doing that was not enough to support the family, and I too had to look for work. Without a car, it's tough to search from place to place, keeping up your smile. Mostly, of course, the jobs we can get are minimum wage with no health insurance, and I defy you to try to support a family of five on that, even if you work ten hours a day, six days a week.

Josiah and I are both halfway healthy but standing on our feet for hours every day makes us so tired, and we don't have time or energy for the kids when we get home. When she can, my sister keeps my baby all day and meets the older kids when school ends. Mom used to do it, but she can't get around as easily as she used to. She's got diabetes pretty bad, and it slows her down. My sis is a big help, but she's got a leg that pains her all the time, and none of her doctors can explain what's going on. They just send her from one doctor to another, and each time she has to make an appointment, waiting in the office for hours before they take her in. I've tried to call for her to get an explanation of what's the problem, but they talk in jargon neither one of us can understand. I've even taken her to the emergency room, but that's an even longer wait, and the kids quickly get ants in their pants and bother all the other sick people.

I'm not sure I even trust all those White doctors. All our people know the stories, mostly from earlier times, but still happening in some places, of women being sterilized for no reason, of men being given syphilis so they can be "observed," like rats in a cage. My great-uncle was one of the kids from Lyles Station, Indiana, where they experimented with radiation treatments on the little kids; he still wears a beanie all the time so as not to reveal the open wound in his skull from when they gave him too much radiation for a five-year-old kid.

My twelve year old worries me; he's getting to be real sassy, and he hangs out with a bad crowd. I think he's skipping classes some days and the teachers at his school just don't like him. When my brother was about nineteen, he started on marijuana. I begged him to stop, but he was at a rebellious age, and one day he got arrested on the street, and even possession of marijuana is a crime. The way the criminal justice system works at all levels from arrest to trial to conviction and incarceration, before he knew it, he was sent to federal prison—one not even near us. When I want to see him, I have to take the train 200 miles, and I can't afford either the time or the cost.

I had a terrible toothache last week that ballooned up my cheek, but the dentist just wouldn't see me if I couldn't pay in advance, and truth is, I could barely pay afterwards. It took two weeks to get an appointment, and I just looked and felt awful all the time. I live in dread of an old appliance breaking down, or the next time my kids grow out of their shoes. We just don't have any money for any unexpected bills.

Some weeks it's hard even to get to a grocery store, and we often stop by the local store on the way home, but we know the quality of their produce and meat is terrible, and it costs more than in the larger chains further away that take us three buses to get to. The kids are complaining of beans and rice, beans and rice, but it's all we can afford. Once a week, we treat ourselves to dinner at McDonald's, and even though I know it's all fat and sugar, it tastes so good!

The public authorities rarely pick up the trash on our street, and it just piles up and blows around over everything. We tell our landlord about plumbing problems, but he doesn't listen, much less come around to solve them. Every time we call, he threatens to sell the property for apartments if we don't stop bothering him. A couple of our neighbors who know how to fix things will help us sometimes, but we hate to be asking for favors all the time. With all the foot-loose teenagers in our neighborhoods, you'd think they could help once in a while, but they'd rather hang out with their gangs. And who knows what the gangs get into, with drugs so easy to get, and even guns, though how do they pay for those? Even so, I'm afraid to let the younger kids out at night; anything might happen to them. And I have to explain to all my kids never-ever to talk back to a cop, and stay away from White neighborhoods, no matter what. I hate to frighten my children with stories of gun-happy policemen, but it is so *urgent* that they know what can and probably will happen to darkie children.

It's just constant . . . one thing after another . . . with no letup in sight. The hardest thing of all, I think, is the way White people look at me—as if I'm scum. For no reason but that my skin is black, they think I'm dumb and worthless. They'd be happier if I disappeared. And they just turn away and pretend I'm not there.

The only thing that helps me keep going is my church. On Sunday mornings, and even most Wednesday nights, we just go in with our arms out to hug each other. We sing songs of joy and sorrow, we cheer on the minister in the sermon, we praise God, we just love each other, and remind each other that God loves us too. That's what helps me endure. And I know that my church belongs to all of us Black folks, just as we belong to God, from times long ago, and times yet to come.

End of Story for Now

I hope you, the reader, have been able to place yourself somewhere in the story above. What it intends to demonstrate is that we have created a polity at all levels in America in which the first encounter a Black person has, for any purpose, is a closed door. Imagine for yourself a life in which, whatever you try to do is met at first with "no." There are a number of possible responses. One may be to give up. But when giving up will impact not only your own life but that of your children, your parents, your own hopes and dreams, you will probably at least try again once. How many "nos" does it take before you throw in the towel? Or try rage, which all too often leads to mutual violence and destruction. Endurance is another way we can manage to focus the strong anger that builds up inside. Sometimes nonviolent direct action is suggested, but that is often infiltrated by violent groups and/or assassins. I encourage you, dear reader, to think for a moment about how you would be likely to respond over time to a world unable or unwilling to see you whole. I full well recognize the audacity of a White woman who has experienced every privilege of Whiteness in America to tell this story. Yet I hope it is true enough about aspects of Black experience in America today that something of it will enable you to recognize and genuinely mourn the ingredients of structural racism found today in every aspect of American society.

Challenge to These Signs of the Times

Kelly Brown Douglas, an African-American Episcopal priest, womanist theologian, the inaugural dean of the Episcopal Divinity School at Union Theological Seminary, and canon theologian at the Washington National Cathedral, writes that the 1619 landing of the slave ship *White Lion* "symbolizes the construction of race as a defining and indelible feature of America's core identity. It stamped Black bodies with the ineradicable identity of subhuman chattel, and signaled the White supremacist foundation upon which America's capitalistic democracy, with all its sociopolitical system and structures, would be built."[33] Dean Douglas points out that the *New York Times* 1619 Project reveals that there has *never* been a genuine effort to redress the wrongs of slavery, which continue in twenty-first-century versions of poverty, mass incarceration, and substandard schools. Her particular concern is the complicit role of Christian churches, which claim a faith "partnering with God to mend an unjust earth and thus to move us toward a more just future," and insists that the future which Christians must build is one "where all human beings are respected as the sacred creations that they are and thereby free to live into the fullness of their sacred creation."[34] Douglas proposes three crucial elements for justice:

(1) *Anamnestic truth-telling,* not merely a retrospective acknowledging of culpability, but speaking the ways the past remains alive in the present, such as White supremacist narratives, ideologies, and constructs that must be dismantled and transformed. Examples in the Episcopal Church include only allowing Whites to be diocesan (governing) bishops, instead creating a powerless category like "suffragan bishop" for Black clerics; using its monotheistic theology to justify slavery and support aggressive Christian protectionist nationalism; and continuing to keep "family secrets" rather the airing and settling with "old ghosts;"

(2) *Fostering a moral identity,* which means naming and denouncing White privilege, rather than passively refusing to confront what it means to be a beneficiary of White supremacy and its legacy, in short, willingness to shed White power, just as Jesus shed his divine power on our behalf (Phil 2:5-8); and

(3) *Proleptic participation*, that is, adjusting the images and icons in our physical churches and in our imagining to include Black and Brown images and patterns as witnesses to God's future, rather than choosing the "easy" way of silence, indifference, and passivity.[35] Business as usual simply will not work anymore.

Cornel West describes this present time in history as "one of *spiritual blackout* and imperial meltdown. The undeniable collapse of integrity, honesty, and decency in our public and private life has fueled even more racial hatred and contempt. The rule of Big Money and its attendant culture . . . have so poisoned our hearts, minds, and souls that a dominant self-righteous . . . smartness, dollars, and bombs thrives with little opposition. . . . Mass distractions on the Internet, TV, and radio push toward an inescapable imperial meltdown."[36] And he goes further to call for "prophetic fightback—a moral and spiritual awakening [to bring about] courageous truth telling and exemplary action by individuals and communities."[37]

West is quite frank in *Race Matters*, specifically in the twenty-fifth anniversary edition (2017), stating that Blacks have been "taught systematically to hate themselves—psychic violence—reinforced by the powers of state and civic coercion—physical violence—for the primary purpose of controlling their minds and exploiting their labor for nearly four hundred years." He further points out that while talking about unemployment, incarceration, hunger, infant mortality, and violent crime is a start, far more important is acknowledging the "murky waters of despair and dread that now flood the streets of black America." As a systematically degraded and oppressed people, Blacks are "hungry for identity, meaning, and self-worth."[38]

That spiritual blackout is the reason I believe resistance to diversity to be the most de-forming of all the issues addressed in section II of this book. It degrades people of color in horrific ways, and it further degrades those who support, ignore, and deny racism. There is no speck of moral fault in those who are degraded, but the log of immorality in the eyes of those who practice racism and speak for racism is blinding (Matt 7:4-5).

At the beginning of this chapter, we saw that diversity in plant and animal life contributes significantly to health and healing. If we take the principle of diversity as a reliable sign of overall health, then we must consider the possibility that White refusal of diversity, White insistence on keeping non-Whites apart and marginalized in many ways, is actually de-forming to *everyone* in American culture, and that White homogeneity may be a major contributing factor to the dis-ease currently afflicting all our people—Black, Brown, Yellow, Red, *and* White.

White America is also suffering a spiritual blackout and is not at ease with itself. Even before the pandemic, which has added considerable distress to all of us, the evidence of dis-ease in America was plentiful. In the past two decades, since 2000, more than 400,000 Americans have died of opioid overdoses. In fall of 2021, the Justice Department obtained an $8.3 billion settlement with Purdue Pharma, maker of OxyContin, high-lighting the widespread problem of overprescribing, diverting, and abusing pain medications while drug manufacturers, pharmacists, and doctors profit.[39] In addition to the 400,000 who have died, another estimated one and one-half million Americans are addicted to opioids. And while suicide rates have fallen around the world, the rate in the US has climbed every year since 1999, increasing 33 percent in the past two decades.[40] Certainly, those numbers include people of color, no doubt in disproportionate numbers; they also include many Whites. Indeed, a report from the American Communities Project that divides US counties into fifteen types, reveals that the "Middle Suburbs," (which are 85 percent White, less di-verse, and less affluent than either the cities or suburbs further out), suffered an average annual rate of 56.3 "deaths of de-spair" over the 2014–2018 period.[41]

And let us not forget that "consumerism" can also be a sign of dis-ease. We Americans have been well taught by our so-phisticated advertising system that we are only "really alive" when spending. The market presents us with a rapid succession of artificially induced and temporarily satisfied desires. When market culture becomes the guiding paradigm for life, meaning itself is undermined.[42] Economic decline, cultural decay, and political lethargy combine to create a widespread sense of helplessness and impotence among us all. American Buddhist psychiatrist John Welwood, noting that depression is currently widespread in American society, calls depression a "loss of heart," an elaborate system of defense to buffer a person from a feeling of being "weighed down" by reality. Depression arises from a basic sense of grief and defeat, similar to what Walter Brueggemann names as a primary result of imperial consciousness, causing people to believe that no other reality is possible.[43]

Psychologist Ann Ulanov has introduced the term "otherwise" to help us welcome diversity. She proposes that, for human flourishing, we must learn to *welcome the other*. Indeed, she postulates that refusal to entertain the other is pathology, which gets us lost in repetition, fragmentation without a center, and falling into a void because there is no "other" where there should be.[44] Congresswoman Ilhan Omar observes that "fear of the 'other'—whether it is someone of a different country of origin, a different race or a different religion—stems . . . from the myth of scarcity":

> This mentality pits minority groups against one another in a fight for scraps, and those who benefit from the status quo are happy to see us distracted and bickering. . . .
> As Toni Morrison put it, "The function, the very serious function of racism is distraction." . . .
> But, as the unrest sweeping the country illustrates, we cannot simply bottle up our pain. . . .
> We need to jettison the zero-sum idea that one person's gain is another's loss.[45]

Ulanov's perspective is that thinking "other-wise" not only frees us from dis-ease and depression, it also opens us to the different and holy Other, and leads our thinking toward "possible" futures, because Godself is the More who seeks to meet us daily and who, with us, mourns injustice.[46]

Interlude C

How Are We Divided?

We are often told that we are a divided country. While I wonder just what that means to each speaker, it does seem that in general, we Americans have lost interest, much less ability, to listen and learn from one another. Let's take a moment to look more honestly at our various divisions, in order to understand how and why it is important to return to genuine conversation with one another. In charts and texts throughout this book, certain fault lines have been described: in the contrast between market culture and human-based culture (chap. 3); in the contrast between empire and earth community (chap. 4); in the contrast between technological/industrial agriculture and climate-sensitive agroecology (chap. 5); and in the contrast between monocultures of the mind and biodiversity, found in human communities as well as plant and animal communities (chap. 6). All these contrasts have underlying themes in common.

Christianity, at least as frequently interpreted, has played a role in creating a one-sided American culture of market, empire, fossil-driven technology, and monocultures of the mind. At first look, this may seem illogical, since Jesus' life itself was certainly not characterized by any of these themes. But one need not look long at the history of Christianity to find a White male God who stands at the top of a hierarchy of values, while women, people of color, the body, and Earth itself stand very near the bottom.

Something has happened along the way that seems to have separated us in fundamental ways, with the effect of turning actual modern American values into death-bringing patterns. We often view modern cultures, with their emphasis on progress, the individual, reason, and science, as a big improvement over traditional cultures that value stability, community, tradition, and faith. And yet today, we see an emergent *new* culture, not yet even sure enough of itself to name itself, except by what it is not. This emergent and challenging new culture is called, at the moment, "postmodern," although there is as yet little understanding of what it might mean in terms of daily life experience. Meanwhile traditional cultures still exist in the world, and many of us still live with the expectations and understandings of modernity, while this new, un-nameable thing is gradually taking up more and more space in contemporary America. I believe that underneath all the other apparent divisions, these major differing cultural values are at the heart of our confusions, dismay, and disagreements.

The French philosopher Jean-Francois Lyotard invented the word "postmodern" in 1984, emphasizing that it signaled "the end of all master stories."[1] Since the "master stories" in question were those predominant in the West, many of us were blind to the idea that they posed a resented hegemony for people whose viewpoints were formed elsewhere or within enclaves with different values from that of our predominant Western master story. Hence, the "middle culture," that of modernity which had generally formed the core of American experience, began to feel it was being challenged from both sides: on the one side, by traditional cultures, and on the other side, by the emergent postmodern culture.

For example, America's master story tells us that "Columbus discovered America," and that master story justified killing those already resident here. Obviously Indigenous peoples took exception to that story. But those peoples seldom had what I call "a seat at the table," or perhaps better, seldom had a voice where public policies were being made and decisions taken. Yet even when a few White women found "seats," Black women rose up to say it was presumptuous of White women to speak for their *womanist* experience, or to Latina *mujerista* wisdom, or even that of Asian women, who claim several seats at the table because in India and Korea, Hong Kong and the Philippines, women's experience is differently contextualized. Furthermore, the tendency of White America strictly to separate church and state is a source of considerable dismay to many Muslims, for whom religious forms of governance are instinctive and even reassuring.[2] At the heart of all these postmodern issues is the matter of whose story will "win," when in fact the great likelihood is that whatever emerges will not be a singular win, but will instead look like a glorious, multicolored gathering of many beautiful stories.

A postmodern world consists of many governing stories and in some sense, all are true because the postmodern world values process and interconnection, multiplicity and interpretations, difference, and even something like mysticism. At first, that may feel like a serious loss to someone steeped in modern or even traditional values. Initially, I may wish to deny the others' truth, as if that were the only way to honor my own. But if I have courage to keep listening, to stay in relationship with the other, I may realize that what I have always known as true must be set alongside a plurality of interacting truths. I may choose to stay with the story I know, but I may also realize that some part of others' stories have new wisdom for me. This involves a huge shift in perspective, and I believe it is exactly where America stands today. (A chart is attached at end of this Interlude, showing primary characteristics of traditional, modern, and postmodern perspectives.)

Living with a diversity of ways of seeing and experiencing the world can call forth new behaviors. I may begin to notice my own experience of difference and perhaps let myself be open to new ideas. I may notice ways I create emotional distance, clinging to things I thought were certain, fearing that my whole self-structure might collapse if I changed even one small thing.

Walter Brueggemann has observed that monotheism is probably a good idea, but if taken too far, it can become reductionist and unidimensional in ways that don't serve anyone. He suggests that pluralism/postmodernism always appears on the human stage after an established, trusted hegemony begins to collapse. The hegemony, the master story, the imperial consciousness that previously claimed absolute obedience is no longer able to repress, deny, or censor other voices. A new moment emerges in which an exchange occurs between the center and the edges, thus making it impossible for the old hegemony to define and hold all power.[3] Brueggemann further suggests that today might indeed be God's season of "scattering the proud in the imagination of their hearts" (Luke 1:51), in the sense of God's utter freedom no longer being channeled solely through traditional patterns of Christendom. Indeed, he reminds us that "God has a rich, complicated, unsettled, lively interiority" that will not be reduced to any one-dimensional thinking.[4]

I believe that in these days, the US and perhaps the world itself is aptly described in this experience of many new and alternative voices seeking a place and a voice at the table where decisions are made, and that God's very self is at the heart of this change. And I take strength from Harvard emeritus professor and developmental psychologist Robert Kegan's view that adult development may evolve even beyond respect for another, who holds an opinion different from mine, to a step Kegan calls "fifth order consciousness." In this new way of thinking, a person or group is willing to suspect their own tendency to feel wholly identified with one side of any opposition, while identifying the other person or group wholly with the other side. With this willingness to see one's own opinion as a possible fixed ideology or orthodoxy, each person in conversation with another can choose to be vulnerable to discovering another world within oneself. Each declines to see oneself as already "complete," and therefore can view disagreement or conflict as an opportunity for self to become more whole, thanks to the genuine offering (alternate opinion) of another.

Kegan suggests that not many of us get to this form of consciousness until midlife, but that a pattern of such openness to one another can develop not just between two or more individuals but also within members or groups within a larger cultural setting.[5]

In other words, the predominance and "correctness" of our previous master story, something that might even be understood as Brueggemann's concept of "totalism," is being challenged on all sides today. The work that is required by all of us is the willingness to be uncertain, and in the poetic words of Ishpriya Mataji, an English religious sister with a doctorate in psychology who lives in an East Indian ashram, to "leave those who can surf the seeming chaos to do so without restrictions and with maximum trust."[6]

Though the American culture today may seem divided and chaotic, God is ahead of us here as always, inviting us into a future not quite yet imagined. Robert W. Radtke, president and CEO of Episcopal Relief and Development, who certainly has an eye on world issues as well as those articulated here in section II, invites us to consider that today we inhabit a liminal space. The word "liminal" comes from the Latin word for "threshold." It suggests the image of standing on a threshold between rooms, having departed from the one behind, but not yet having arrived at the one ahead, a place neither here nor there, but in between. The word liminal came into English through the work of anthropologist Victor Turner, who studied the rites that young men or women must endure before they were fully recognized as members of a tribe, and which were considered a liminal period. As Radtke notes and as we might imagine, such periods are typically full of anxiety; we would like more certainty ahead of time about the outcome. The irony, of course, is that by definition, liminal spaces are "precisely where transformation can take place—an opening where we have let go of the past and [are] reaching toward the future, without fully knowing what that future holds . . . We act by faith."[7]

Section II has identified some of the principal problems facing the US today. Brueggemann's theory has given us a way to think about how to release our typical viewpoints, even about our religion, which often seems to become tightly tied to our political and economic aspirations, allowing us to call that whole muddle "an imperial consciousness" that is squeezing the life out of our culture. In contrast, Brueggemann's theory has also given us language from which we can launch serious challenges to "the way things are." In section III, the gifts of prophetic imagination and Benedictine spirituality are applied to offer us ways to live creatively in the unknown, embodied ways of ancient truths that give us resources to meet the opportunities of today.

Table created by Norvene Vest, with guidance from:

Gilles Deleuze and Felix Guattari, *A Thousand Plateaus: Capitalism and Schizophrenia, Vol. 2*, trans. Brian Massumi (Minneapolis: University of Minnesota Press, 1987). Deleuze and Guattari use the terms "rhizome" and "rhizomatic" to describe theory and research that allows for multiple, non-hierarchical entry and exit points in data representation and interpretation. They oppose it to an arborescent (hierarchic, tree-like) conception of knowledge, which works with dualist categories and binary choices. A rhizome works with planar and trans-species connections, while an arborescent model works with vertical and linear connections.

Nathan D. Mitchell, *Meeting Mystery* (Maryknoll, NY: Orbis Books, 2006).

Susan R. Bordo, *The Flight to Objectivity: Essays on Cartesianism & Culture* (Albany, NY: State University of New York Press, 1987).

Chart: Primary Characteristics of Traditional, Modern, and Postmodern Cultures

Traditional Cultures	Modern Cultures	Postmodern Cultures	
Stability	Innovation/ Progress	Process	
Regularity	Novelty	The Many	
Hierarchy	Individual	Networks	
Familiarity	Structure and form, e.g., "nouns"	Movement, e.g. "verbs"	
Faith/Revelation	Science/ Discovery	Poetry/Metaphor	Liminal Space
Repetition	Reason	The Indeterminate Sublime, both Terrible and Wondrous	↓
"Magic"	Science/ Explanation	Participation	Unknown Future
Universal Truths/ Master Story	Empiricism, Separation, Analysis	Interpretation, Relationships, Interchange	
Authority	Skepticism	Mutuality in Knowledge Creation	
Cosmology	Autonomy	Otherness	
	Aboreal (tree-like)	Rhizomatic (crabgrass)	

Section III

Formative Challenge to Public Policies

CHAPTER SEVEN

Lament and *Conversatio*

Strengthen the weak hands
  and make firm the feeble knees.
Say to those who are of a fearful heart,
  Be strong, do not fear!
Here is your God. . . .

Then the eyes of the blind shall be opened,
  and the ears of the deaf unstopped;
then the lame shall leap like a deer,
  and the tongue of the speechless sing for joy.

(Isa 35:3-4a, 5-6a)

Section I on America's promise explored the spiritual roots of American democracy, as well as two missed opportunities to reclaim the fullness of our country's promise. Section II laid out four major policies that have been and are now de-forming our original promise. Section III now draws attention to possible ways we might together claim a new future, restoring our country's original promise, through prophetic lament, Benedictine return/conversion, and ongoing spiritual formation.

What can we do? That is the American question! We are the "can do" people, confident that with our intelligence and technology, we can defeat any problem. Just now, however, the future depends less on our *doing* than on our *being*. The first step in moving out of our de-forming cultural patterns is to witness clearly and claim our own responsibility in co-creating

141

present conditions. Recall Abraham Heschel's prophetic statement, "the prophets remind us of the moral state of a people: few are guilty but all are responsible."[1] Likely most readers are not *directly* creating the patterns of de-formation described in section II, but as citizens we are responsible for the overall moral state of our country. Too often, too many of us look the other way, are not concerned if something doesn't affect us directly, or even are content to rest in the benefits we inherit at the expense of many others. All this is short-term thinking. One of my own teachers, who was a teenager in Holland during the time of Hitler's rise to power, tells the story of her mother's decision to hide a Jewish girl in their home at a time when her husband was away fighting the German army. Her mother's friends criticized her mother severely for putting her young daughter (my teacher) at risk, if the German soldiers "happened to" discover the Jewish girl in their home. My teacher's mother replied, "If anyone is at risk, we all are at risk. I choose the side of compassion."

Where Is God?

The America we live in is not particularly a compassionate place. Hierarchy, dominance, and profit are the controlling factors. If we are not yet at risk of being repressed by these factors, it is likely we will be, as they continue unchecked. In America, faith communities have often joined to influence public policy movements toward compassion. Current polls show that most denominations are declining in membership, so there is also some decline in the public policy engagement of worshiping communities themselves. However, a very high percentage of Americans say they believe in God or some form of Higher Power, though they often do not participate in faith communities where they might spiritually be formed together for witness and challenge. Of course, many diverse nonprofit groups often come together in concern about specific public policies, such as climate change. Yet, as suggested above, when people are numbed and distressed about prevalent conditions, it is difficult to arouse energy. Many of us find ourselves seeking comfort in these difficult times and avoiding challenge.

Given that the aim of this book is the restoration of a significant role for the sacred in public policy, and given the fog about "realistic" alternatives that any totalism creates, I believe it necessary to begin this section with some reflections on God. As we saw in Moses' story of leading the Hebrews out of Egypt, the deciding factor was God's unlimited freedom. Therefore, my sense is that as an American people, we need some conviction that a God exists whom we can depend upon. In some respects, that is ironic, given the increasing movement of some American religious practice toward what we have called "Constantinian Christianity," meaning a form of Christianity drawn away from its seminal beliefs and values, rather to be absorbed into national goals, as was the case in the Rome of Emperor Constantine. This movement brings with it religious expressions linked more tightly to our de-forming national aims than to divine guidance. Yet my own religious experience assures me that, even in these confusing times, a vital community of fidelity to God's Spirit remains, one that encompasses many expressions of authentic Christian faith.

My personal spiritual formation is grounded in the Christian faith, and my thoughts about God are formed by Christian Scripture, tradition, sacraments, and theology, as well as by reason and affection. I am an Episcopal laywoman and a Benedictine oblate of a Catholic women's monastery in Virginia. I also call myself a feminist theologian, grounded not only in serious study of religious history but also serious study of contemporary theology. Rooted in Christian heritage and community, I receive guidance, assurance, and a sense of being "at home" in Christian mythology. For me, the term "mythology" refers to a dimension of truth going well beyond what can be spoken in prose. I am acutely aware that traditional, and especially literal, interpretations of Christian stories often fail to be meaningful and sometimes, are even hurtful to many in today's world. Hence, I believe the theologian's task is to make vivid the ongoing intersection between the deep basic truths about God's presence within human history and the lives we actually lead in these days.

Here's how I understand the sacred. The basic reality about God is more than we humans can ever know; thus the core "fact" is that we remain always uncertain. I am fond of saying that all our language about God limps, that is, every effort to "explain" God is incomplete and even possibly wrong. The method science employs is simply inadequate when applied to God; there will never be "proof" in the way we've come to expect it. What we understand of God generally depends upon whatever we understand of our world, whatever we understand about knowledge and its limits. Hence, our ideas about God will change with our capacities and experience. That does not necessarily mean that the old understandings are wrong, just that some of them are limited by human capabilities at the time. But because our religious understandings are often wrapped in stories and metaphors, even the old ways are multivalent, that is, capable of new interpretations more meaningful in changed times.

C. S. Lewis, professor, novelist, and master of metaphor, notes in his essay called "Transposition" that critics and sceptics certainly have a case for the nonexistence of God, because of "the obvious continuity between things which are admittedly natural (say, eating and drinking) and things which, it is claimed, are spiritual (mass/eucharist)."[2] Lewis is suggesting that "our emotional life is 'higher' than the life of our sensations—not, of course, morally higher, but richer, more varied, more subtle,"[3] because the same physical sensations have to represent more than one emotion, in effect, transposing or adapting from a poorer to a richer medium. His particular metaphor that captures my imagination is that when one tries to translate from a language that has a large vocabulary into a language that has a smaller vocabulary, it will be necessary to use several words, which still may not communicate the nuances available in the larger vocabulary. In just the same way, Lewis urges that what is happening in the lower medium (natural sensations) can be understood only if we know the higher medium (the spiritual). In other words, what we experience of God through the Spirit can never be fully understood by another person until he or she has some experience themselves of the Spirit. This is perhaps a strange claim, and it is not meant to assert that "spiritual things" are higher or better than "natural ones." Rather, it suggests that we humans can resist or refuse to acknowledge the presence of God, because it is costly. We are "small" in relation to God, yet deeply beloved. Love changes us.

It is important to bring God into this final section on possibilities open to us, because, just as Moses discovered centuries ago, our own good intentions are not strong enough by themselves for what is needed today until they are strengthened and guided by God. I invite you to come to these last two chapters, holding lightly your own present vision of who God is and open to what God can do. Love itself will meet us.

Lament: The Prophetic Cry

It is no accident that the word "lament" so frequently surfaces these days in our media. The first step in dealing with our de-formation as a culture is an honest facing of our complicity by avoidance and denial about the signs of de-formation revealed in section II. If we witness without denial and are honest, lament naturally comes, in tears and groans and prayers. Lament is not so much a doing as it is a quality of being. It feels like suffering. It feels like pain. How could God possibly be involved in this?

Theologian Soong-Chan Rah defines lament as "the appropriate liturgical, ecclesial, spiritual response to the reality of pain, suffering, and crisis in the world."[4] Lament requires that we acknowledge the reality of suffering and pain and express an appropriate response of communal grief. The book of

Psalms in the Bible offers many types of lament, and always lament is directed to God, asking either for help or forgiveness. Of course, it is possible to skip this step, moving quickly toward solutions, as we understandably moved quickly to produce a vaccine for COVID-19, without finding time to reflect on the state of our health care system, the suffering already falling disproportionately on marginalized groups of our people, and whether and how a functional vaccine could be distributed and/or accepted. Avoiding reflection and lament, we might also ignore problems, stoically thinking that since God is in control, problems will solve themselves and everything will be fine. Taking that option, we end up justifying the status quo.[5] In some cases, lament blames God for one's pain, in accordance with the pattern in our consumerist culture, keeping *ourselves* as the agenda, and blaming God further or abandoning God altogether, if immediate help is not provided.

When we do genuinely acknowledge not just our own, but widespread suffering in the culture at large, lament can take several forms, including confession, despair, and protest. Laments of confession can be individual or corporate, acknowledging one's own responsibility, sometimes realizing that one has forsaken God and has benefited from and perhaps even perpetuated immoral paradigms of the dominant culture. Laments of despair cry out to God with an overwhelming sense of isolation and defeat. In despair, those who are taking the brunt of the suffering may call out to question God. How can this happen? Why? Where is meaning in this? C. S. Lewis once commented that we live in a universe that contains much that is bad and apparently meaningless, but at the same time contains creatures like ourselves who somehow *know* it is bad and meaningless. God did not have to make us this way. What is the point?[6]

Continuing to cry to God with anguish and doubt, gradually we may "awaken to a different kind of relationship with a mysterious other whose freedom and power transcend anything manageable or handy."[7] When we protest to God, we yet remain in *some relationship* with the God of the Gospel "who is in, with, and under the crisis leading to the new creation."[8] Slowly, our relationship with God may change, and we begin to see things differently. Rabbi Nahum Ward Lev, in Walter Brueggemann's book *The Virus as a Summons to Faith: Biblical Reflections in a Time of Loss, Grief, and Uncertainty,* speaks of a new creation emerging from a new human-divine relationship: "Radical newness is not pain-free for God. Nor is such a birthing pain-free for us. A new world will come with a cost, the cost of acknowledging that our old creation has failed and is dysfunctional, and must be relinquished, renounced and repented. Such letting go is painful. Nevertheless, we are summoned to this relinquishing and rebirthing. . . . Our covenant with Living Presence gifts us with God's mercy and tenacious solidarity, a steadfast love that is strong enough to see us through."[9]

Let's stop for a moment to integrate this idea, that a necessary preparation for humility and repentance is lament. In ongoing lament we gradually realize our own incapacity to make a difference, unless we acknowledge God's freedom as an essential part of the new creation. God's involvement creates a corresponding freedom in ourselves that will be needed for the hard work of letting go of the "cherished idols" or points of view that have so far impeded our role in co-creating the emergent newness.

In a remarkable commentary on the biblical book of Lamentations, theologian Kathleen M. O'Connor emphasizes the power of the *missing voice,* that is, while each voice in that book embodies some aspect of the suffering that belongs to the whole community, *God's voice is never heard.* God does not answer the intense sorrow of the people. Reflecting, O'Connor applauds that fact as one that highlights and strengthens all the other voices. In today's world, "to gain a voice means to come into the truth of one's history corporately and individually, to recover one's life, to acquire moral agency by naming

one's world . . . . Lamentations embodies postmodern understandings of truth, . . . that no single voice, theory, or theology
is able to encompass the multiplicity of human experience."[10]
The vacant space, the missing voice, leaves a well of unrealized
longing, forcing people to *see the wreckage* of the existing symbolic narrative. As it stands, Lamentations ruptures life, for
the old story has failed, and a new one has not yet arrived. The
moment is *liminal*, a threshold time. The people have been
thrust out of the previous narrative, but the new has not yet
fully appeared, much as we feel today.

In the last two years in the United States and indeed around
the world, many of us have experienced the loss of any predictable future. In a sense, the pandemic and shelter-at-home
restrictions have left us in a time of confusion and uncertainty.
We yearn for a return to "the normal," but realistically we
know that the "normal" we knew before the pandemic will
never return. In our time, O'Connor and Brueggemann help
us move *beyond our denial* that the communal future will necessarily bring the return we seek. Facing our denial, we learn to
claim our grief and sorrow about what is bound to be a shat-
tered narrative. And ironically, when we authentically claim
the loss of the old broken narrative, we actually begin to participate in the creation of a new one.

How do we lament? We need to get out of our heads, to let
our feelings emerge, to move our bodies, allowing space for
whatever emotionally and physically carries an expression of
sorrow. In the US, we have lost approximately 986,000 lives[11]
to COVID-19, more Americans than died on the battlefields of
World War I, World War II, and the Vietnam War combined.
President Biden ordered American flags at federal buildings
throughout the country to be lowered for five days, saying,
"We have to resist becoming numb to the sorrow. We have to
resist viewing each life as a statistic or a blur."[12] To receive this
trauma at the feeling level is both frightening and liberating,
for through lament we "learn to see the great events of history
from below . . . from the perspective of the suffering."[13]

A group of pastors in the Los Angeles area seeking to understand and engage the way racism had played out locally recently took a bus together to the Watts neighborhood, which has suffered not only from COVID-19 but in various ways disproportionate to their numbers over recent decades. The group came to a stop at the exhibit of a noose hanging from a tree. Their guide, Tina Watkins, began to sing "Strange Fruit." The group stood silently as the words of the song unfolded around them.

> Southern trees bearing strange fruit
> Blood on the leaves and blood at the roots
> Black bodies swinging in the southern breeze
> Strange fruit hanging from the poplar trees.

Many in the group were moved to tears in that moment of memory, emotion, and truth telling.[14]

The group of pastors found that lament both gives voice to the pain and anger felt especially by many people of color and also challenges those who need to repent for their complicity in the status quo. Later, one of the group's Black members invited everyone into an experience of bodily lament, calling groups of eight people at a time to join each other on a stage, asking each one spontaneously to choose both an action and a sound to express what lament felt like for them, and repetitively to carry out that action and sound, until all on stage were moving and sounding again and again. Although many felt "way out of" their comfort zone, the energy on stage was electric as all expressed deep emotions and groaning toward God. Though somewhat reluctant at first, each participant gradually grasped the power of voice and body much more directly than words alone could offer. One participant described the experience as "a collective expression of God's heart, the groanings, the sound, the pain and the sorrow."[15]

How do we lament? We face the truth of what our country has become, and we receive it fully into our thoughts, emotions, and bodies. Directing our grief to God, we claim our individual voices and perhaps join with others who take time to grieve as we do, in addition to finding solutions. We allow ourselves to be changed as we honor the losses.

Lament: Benedictine *Conversatio*

In the process of lamenting to and with God, we are *allowing ourselves to be changed*. This is the next essential part of lament. We may be crying out to God who does not answer, thinking that the only remedy will come when God *does answer*; yet something about the very dynamic of calling out to God *changes us.* The first step of lament is prophetic in the sense of causing us to bear witness, to see clearly, as we find our own voice raised *prophetically* to and with God. And then lament brings us Benedictine *"conversatio,"* which might be phrased as *repentance* or even *turning* (over a new leaf), but which I prefer to call *ongoing conversion of heart.*

Brief Excursus on Benedictine Life in the World

You may be aware that in today's world, there are approximately as many Benedictine oblates as there are vowed Benedictine monastics. In the Middle Ages, when Benedictine monasteries were in their prime, many nearby families chose to give one or more of their children to be raised and educated by the monks and nuns. The "gift" of these children was called an oblation, an offering, in the same way that today gifts of money to support the church are sometimes called "alms and oblations." Sometimes the given children would stay permanently with the monastic community as adults, but that was not necessarily the case.

Today, adults of faith who live in the common world outside a monastery, may nevertheless wish to establish a closer relationship with a particular monastery by what is still called an "oblation," an offering of themselves to live the Gospel in accordance with some of the principles of Benedict's Rule, "insofar as their state in life permits." For some years in the US, this generally meant helping out in whatever way laity could, such as working in the monastery's reception area, the library, the kitchen on special occasions, or the bookstore. Gradually, oblates began to want to share some of the spiritual life of the monastics, again in accord with constraints of living in the world, and monasteries began to develop guidelines to assist "worldly" folk to build a stronger spiritual life.

Gradually, even those practices helped to deepen the desire of oblates, as they/we began to sense that monastics "had" something important, not only in their spiritual practices, but also in the way they "saw" the world. Benedict himself, and many of his spiritual sons and daughters, seem to manage to be relatively free of cultural baggage, that is, they are more apt than others of us to notice the difference between Gospel principles and cultural claims. I suspect that may be one of the reasons why the Rule continues to be fruitful across so many times and places. Benedictine voices stand as ongoing witness to the truths that last when surface things change. They stand as a challenge to the presumptions of any age.

I believe this witness is the essence of the Benedictine value of being "on the margins." At best, Benedictines avoid the whirlpool, the seductive center of society's fads, not primarily by being "separate" but by their commitment to be a witness. And they do this with the clarity of vision brought through their regular disciplines of vulnerable presence to God. Chief among these disciplines is one aspect of the vows made upon joining a Benedictine community, whether as a monastic or as an oblate, a promise called by Benedict *conversatione morum suorum* (RB 58.17). It is probably a mistake in Latin that is untranslatable, but so central to Benedictine life that it is often simply stated in English as "fidelity to the monastic way of life." I understand it to mean "offering myself to an ongoing process of inner conversion." In this promise, we express our willingness daily to surrender our cherished ideas and projects to the possibility that God will surprise us with something previously unimaginable. *Conversatio* is a way of speaking of the daily dying to self that is essential to ongoing rebirth into Christ.

It is tempting to abbreviate that strange vow simply as conversion, a "turning around" or *metanoia*, in the Greek. Dom Timothy, OSB, of Belmont Abbey in Hereford, England, suggests that an even better Greek word might be *epistrephein*, because that word carries the sense that *God* is spinning us, rather than the implication in *metanoia* that we humans initiate the turning. Even if it does seem disorienting, I welcome the idea of dancing with God! But I resist the singular term "conversion" because it is too often associated with a once-in-a-lifetime event, whereas I think of *conversatio* as a daily commitment. Francis Benedict, OSB, of St. Andrew's Abbey in Valyermo, CA, thinks of *conversatio* as dynamic because it is actually an ongoing dialogue with God about the way one is living, a dialogue that gradually may bring a person to Christ-like maturity.

What is "dying to self?" It is not about a passive surrender, but it is about surrender. Before moving toward that surrender, it is well to have developed a sense of self strong enough to be capable of receiving and accepting love. Yet in general the construction of that strong self includes a certain amount of "make-believe." That is, we often present to the world a sort of mask suggesting that we are invulnerable, all-put-together, needing nothing or no one, because, as Sister Joan Chittister wrote, "we all know down deep [that the world] is a very vulnerable place. . . . We fear vulnerability. It takes a great deal of living to discover that, actually, vulnerability comes to us more as friend than as enemy. . . . Vulnerability is the gift given to us . . . [to enable us to] know ourselves to be human—full of humility, full of love, full of hope. It is the stuff of great spiritual insight, deep spiritual experience, and boundless spiritual bonding."[16]

As I more and more learn the monastic gift of practicing *conversatio*, I sense that its purpose is to help me be persistent

in my aspiration toward God even and especially in the face
of daily struggles. God meets me most reliably at the point of
my temptations and doubts and discomforts. Whenever I trip
over yet another example of my hardness of heart, I learn that
such realizations are not meant to cause me discouragement
and despair but are actually signs of deepening invitation to
live in and with Christ's own life, just here and now. As I pray
with Benedict's Rule, I am astonished by Benedict's ability to
hold in tension two elements of the spiritual life that are often
divided: (1) the need for our own disciplined work of growing
honest self-awareness—the ascetical side; and (2) the ever-
present reality of God's abundant love for us—the mystical
side. In the Rule, these two ingredients are always in intimate
relationship with each other. Our spiritual disciplines are not
to be motivated by fear and guilt, but by love and joy, and our
reception of God's generous grace deepens our desire to re-
move all that separates us from that loving and powerful
relationship.[17]

Nevertheless, *conversatio* is not a comforting process. It is
about being broken and renewed, being overwhelmed and
raised up, suffering and confused because things are changing
and we can't figure anything out. We are no longer in control,
but now are in the hands of the living God who always shatters
our expectations and surpasses our imaginations. Theologian
Raimundo Panikkar suggests that, unlike the angels who completely fulfill their nature simply by their existence, we humans
must spend a lifetime acquiring full humanness. By and large,
the human longing for More Than the merely natural will
generally discover helpful means within religious traditions.
Although there exist many religions and many means, all of
them correspond to an inherent "human wellspring which can
be channeled in different degrees of purity and awareness."
However, *all* those means will "require a rupture, a break, a
shift in the tissues of the human heart. . . . Only when the
heart is broken open can one begin anew by setting out to make
it whole again in a wider and deeper way than before. . . .

Seen from the far shore, from the new life, it is not a broken but a renewed heart."[18]

Cultural Lament and Turning: Living into the Pattern of Christ's Life

The personal pattern for lament is also social one. When we personally or communally insist on controlling things, on keeping them in a familiar and comfortable order, we limit the possible outcomes to those we can imagine. But the great issues of our times require something quite new, quite beyond existing models, quite beyond the perspectives we have always maintained. In this sense, our whole American community needs to have our hearts broken! We can sense that our world is trembling in anticipation of great change, change that will no doubt include the loss of much that we have known and indeed loved, and yet will also include the powerful purposes of the living God. Many of our major institutions are already showing signs of growing cracks, and the coming changes may require their rupture and their loss, as well. *Conversatio* is about the paschal mystery of death as the opening to new life, as each and all of us live it out daily for a lifetime.

The call that emerges from the unique Benedictine commitment to *conversatio* involves both witness and challenge not only to oneself, but also to our American culture, which needs and can benefit greatly by more honest self-awareness and respect for the sacred. The call of *conversatio* to individuals, and also to communities of faith, is *not* primarily to tranquility but rather, to willingness to be sorely tried and passionately caring. Our call is not to have certainty, and not even to have "success," but rather to be foolish for God, for we are invited to be a people willing to rely (or at least seeking to rely) on the living God for yesterday, today, and tomorrow. *Conversatione morum suorum* is a commitment not just for individuals, but for a whole people willing to do the tough work of building for a better world.

In an earlier book of Walter Brueggemann's on the psalms, he picks up on the theme of how to be and what to do in liminal times of uncertainty between cultural paradigm shifts. Brueggemann observes that the whole collection of the Psalter "is not for those whose life is one of uninterrupted continuity and equilibrium," adding that "most of us who think our lives are that way have been numbed, desensitized, and suppressed so that we are cut off from what is in fact going on in our lives." We must first consider "the experiences of disorientation and reorientation that characterize human life and *that are the driving power* of the Psalms." In general, the psalms, and especially the lament psalms, are not courteous or polite; "they are religious only in the sense that they are willing to articulate this chaos to the very face of the Holy One." The psalms assure us that we are not meant to hide our anger and our pain, but to "submit it openly and trustingly" to God.[19] The psalms invite us to open our hearts to God about what the personal and cultural situations truly are.

Social Justice and Prayer

Many thoughtful observers now press for the necessary complementarity of social justice and contemplative prayer. Jim Wallis, the founder of *Sojourners*, created a podcast in early April 2020, anticipating the church's annual preparation for Easter and reflecting on the COVID-19 pandemic that was then beginning to spread rapidly around the world. Wallis's podcast was an interview with Richard Rohr, a Franciscan Catholic friar, about the increasingly dominant "politics of deceit" in the United States. Both agreed that there was an urgent need to rewire the current American delusional mind that so insistently refuses to acknowledge the absence of justice and peace among us. Such rewiring would newly root our common American vision in the ground of the sacred. Rohr spoke of his conviction that Jesus came to reveal *the shape of reality* and how it works. While we may acknowledge this shape of reality in Jesus' death and resurrection (that death, especially of distorted vision, is often the necessary opening to new life), we may hope it doesn't come close to home. But Benedictine *conversatio* also follows the pattern of dying to the old in order to be open to new life. Easter in ecclesial memory and in practical, current time, is not about going back to normal; it is about clearing the space of delusion and denial to make room for genuine renewal.

In his book on addiction, Rohr urges us to see our reality for what it is, in particular, that our society is showing all the signs of classic addiction. He suggests that it is helpful to see sin, like addiction, as a *disease* instead of a punishable moral weakness.[20] "Every culture and every institution embodies shared and agreed-upon addictions. These are often the hardest to heal because they do not look like addictions, because we have all agreed to be compulsive about the same things and blind to the same problems. . . . Some form of alternative consciousness is the only freedom from cultural lies and the self it creates."[21]

However, as we have seen, the route to the alternative consciousness necessary for healing and wholeness is *by way of intentional struggles with our own contradictions, conflicts, inconsistencies, inner confusion* and the like. Like Benedict, Rohr teaches that the sadness and grief we experience coming face to face with our own weaknesses and failures can only be borne when we have learned to be confident in a Greater Love. Since we rarely experience God directly jumping in to correct and improve us or others, how do we gain that confidence in this Greater Love? Rohr observes that too often Christian churches "over-spiritualize" faith and thus have little to say about "how God actually loves the world into wholeness." He urges that we find our way through this dilemma by following Jesus through the last week of his life, thus learning that God is somehow in our suffering, participating in full solidarity with the world, giving suffering a meaning.[22] We join God, and God joins us, in divine suffering. *This* is the God we meet in our spiritual practice, the One who joins us in *every* experience and loves us just there. Hence, "the goal of the spiritual life is not the perfect avoidance of moral weakness, which is not possible anyway, but the struggle itself, the encounter and the wisdom that comes with it."[23]

Ishpriya Mataji has committed herself to the path of wisdom, earning a PhD in psychology in Britain and subsequently choosing daily life in an ashram in India. She was invited to write an article for *The Way* journal on the topic "How should religious life be re-visioned in a Church that no longer sees 'consecration' as the sole preserve of community-based celibates?" After struggling with the topic for some time, Ishpriya admitted to some pain in the growing conviction that in our present world, the time had passed in which that question could make any sense, much less be answered. She knew that when pain is lived, neither rejected nor exaggerated, it eventually leads to a fuller life and more profound meaning. Accordingly, Ishpriya observed that the current attempt to build interim measures that carry the seeds of the future is doomed to failure. "We have said farewell to much of Newtonian physics and stand now in a quantum world-view which gives us a greater appreciation of the role of chaos in creation." Ishpriya adds that the "violent rending apart of our times is vibrating with the apocalyptic cry: 'Behold, I make all things new' (Rev 21:5). *New*, not adapted, not re-organized, not revised, but totally new. . . . To be able to hear that voice, the voice of the One Who alone speaks with authority, means that we have already grown comfortable with uncertainty, that we have come to accept chaos and confusion as prerequisites for a deeper understanding of the wisdom of evolution. . . . Contemporary scientists and contemporary mystics speak of an evolution of *consciousness*."[24]

When our vision is clear, what we see in our culture is what has been called "a dying world," according to Debra Dean Murphy.[25] Similarly, Dennis Slattery observes that "our prevailing belief systems in government, finance, housing, American dream, education, the earth herself and others are collapsing. Let things fall apart and allow the center not to hold—then we can renew our culture."[26] A friend of mine, now an Episcopal bishop, spoke with a church congregation about how to grow and adapt to changing demographics. She knew they expected a talk about embracing the interracial reality of the next generation in order to survive, but instead she told them that death is part of life. She said that, as Christians, we cannot run away from the reality of death and the change that it invites us into. "While that is a hard reality to embrace, some of our major institutions are in fact falling apart. It looks grim and tragic; but might it also suggest new openings and possibilities?!"[27]

Another perspective may provide context for such observations. Ewert Cousins has identified tribal culture as a time of *preaxial* consciousness, collective in experience, with no sense of an individual identity. In contrast, a sense of being a separate "self" was the central characteristic of the *axial* period of consciousness, co-terminus with the advent of the great religions, dissolving all sense of oneness with others or creation. Now there are intuitions that human consciousness is developing the capacity to express simultaneously *both* an experience of oneness, of union of being with creation, *and* an equally acute awareness of individual identity, of a unique self. This new form of consciousness can be called *mystical consciousness*.[28]

Mystical awareness discerns the indwelling presence of the Mystery, God, in all this. Ishpriya continues her reflections:

> The core experience is that *all* is in essence *sacred* because all is created and held in being by God. . . . The spiritual discipline which develops this consciousness is a reverent attention to every event, a fierce loving and a universal detachment. The demanding training in how to care and not to care . . . cannot be avoided. . . . The God the mystics encounter is an untamed, wild God, who upsets all their expectations and destroys all order as they have known it. . . . They must be a community of broken people, painfully honest, vulnerable, undomesticated, the faithful who have always been marginalized by the establishment.[29]

Here, too, we encounter the integration of profound spiritual discipline with the very life of God, bringing an acute sense of some aspects of life dying, while unanticipated new aspects are emerging in the full freedom of God.

How like these observations are to Brueggemann's insights about the remarkable exodus of the Hebrew people from the imperial consciousness of Egypt's Pharoah. Moses' time in the desert had formed his spirit into the service of the compelling freedom of God, creating an event that only a prayerful prophetic consciousness could imagine. If we are willing to bear the losses involved in consenting to our wild, untamed God, we too can make an exodus together into an astonishingly new world.

Here I share my own vision about how to look at today's American culture with hope. I too believe that many of our major institutions are collapsing. We need only think of the deadlocks in our current Congress, or of the fact that basic standards in today's schools tend to take the shape of one-size-fits-all, or that hospital policies are often designed by MBAs employed in insurance firms with little or no concern for individual human care. Watching such matters unfold, it is easy to feel helpless and despairing. But I believe that the truth of the death and resurrection metaphoric narrative at the heart of Christianity is also a characteristic pattern found in personal and cultural history. What looks to be, even what feels like, death often *precedes* new growth.

The new physics confirms a similar pattern in chaos theory. The physicists are telling us that what appears to be chaos, something we have always considered the predecessor to entropy, may in fact be a form of re-creation. Scientists chart chaotic movements showing that eventually chaos can produce a completely new and more fully adequate pattern for future events. Sometimes chaos produces collapse; but in an astonishingly high percentage of occasions, it produces new patterns that are capable of embracing more comprehensive and complex realities.

We live in a time when thoughtful people are witnesses to collapsing institutions, institutions that often collapse by imploding, bursting inwards, because that's where the decay is. We cannot prop them up from the outside because that will not stop an implosion. At this point, what is needed is not simply tinkering with the system; it needs to be dismantled and transformed. Brueggemann suggests we imitate the compassion of Jesus, because the one quality of relationship that is unpermitted in empires is compassion. In such a situation, compassion can be both a personal emotional reaction, and also a public criticism in which together we dare to act on our concern, even experiencing numbness and blindness, making visible the odd normality that today has become business as usual.[30] In the meantime, Pastor Otis Moss III sharpens the alternatives for us, asking, "Will believers in Jesus [answer this moment by deciding] to be chaplains for the empire or prophets to the nation?"[31]

CHAPTER EIGHT

Our Task of Prophetic Imagination

Sing praises to the LORD, O you his faithful ones,
and give thanks to his holy name.
For [God's] anger is but for a moment;
his favor is for a lifetime.
Weeping may linger for the night,
but joy comes with the morning. . . .

You have turned my mourning into dancing;
you have taken off my sackcloth
and clothed me with joy,
so that my soul may praise you and not be silent.

(Ps 30:4-5, 11-12a)

Chapter 7 set out the nature of the task to which we are called if we choose to become agents of prophetic imagination in times like these. As we have seen, this is not by any means an easy task: It calls for us to develop an intense self-honesty, vulnerability, and willingness to be changed, not only in our personal self-understanding and daily habits but also as citizens of our country and the world. We see that our work in some ways requires a kind of daily "dying," modeled literally by Jesus, but for us more in terms of accepting necessary losses and releasing cherished assumptions. We risk doing so with confidence that through Christ, some as yet invisible new life is emerging through our faithful participation in a courageous community.

This final chapter invites us specifically to take up the work of prophetic imagination, grounded in a clear vision of what

America is becoming, and sharing the pathos of God in lament and openness to God's radically new vision. The presence/experience/call of God is the first step toward dismantling cultural and political de-formation; our faithful response is the second; and formative participation in community life is the third. But *how* do we experience God's call and *what is the shape* of a faithful and participative response? In light of my primary foundations in prophetic imagination and Benedictine spirituality, I understand faithful response to center in spiritual discipline or spiritual formation, including communal formation and not just that of individuals. That is to say, effective response to God's call involves our openness to change.

Ishpryia Mataji speaks of a spiritual discipline that develops a "mystical consciousness" that teaches us "how to care and not to care."[1] What can that mean, to care and not to care? I think care means real compassion for everyone who needs help, at the same time with awareness that those to whom we reach out also have gifts that will be of help to us in return. This is not the "high road" of charity but rather, the respectful walk of mutual dignity. And "not to care" likely means we are not to be too heavily invested in our own preferred outcomes, for ultimately this is God's work. Finally, this task is immensely strengthened when we are participating in a community where everyone is committed to similar principles and similar challenges. All of this is difficult work, if not frankly irritating to our egos (which, of course, is part of the work).

There are three linked dimensions to the task of prophetic imagination. From the one dimension is the call and the strength of God; and from the second is our own faithful response. The third dimension, a notion of shared "mystical consciousness" that is a gift of the Holy Spirit, links all three. We'll explore them one at a time.

The God Who Calls

First, let us return to Brueggemann's insight about the full and astonishing freedom of God, who was the source of the "impossible" exodus of the Hebrew people from slavery in Egypt. I use the term "impossible" deliberately, because the long-ago Hebrew people, like most Americans today, thought significant change impossible. Recall that one of the primary effects of imperial consciousness is "recurring practices that serve to totalize the claim of the regime, taking up all the social space and allowing for no alternative possibility."[2] Imperial consciousness, described in Interlude A and chapter 4 as our contemporary American cultural situation, pretends that no other way is possible than its dominant, controlling hierarchy that claims our very souls. The free God whom Moses served made possible what had been thought to be impossible in Egypt! Moses accepted the task of prophetic imagination, obedient to God's call, to provide energy for hope, to cut through the numbness, and to penetrate the self-deception of imperial consciousness. Moses' task of prophetic imagination *is also ours today*, that is, to provide energy for hope, to cut through the numbness, and to penetrate the self-deception of imperial consciousness so that the real God and the sacred again become visible and empowering for our people.

Today, can we believe in and rely on the God of Moses? Both imaginative prophecy and Benedictine spirituality answer "Yes!" How do they come to this affirmation? Chapter 1 suggested that both of these ancient sources lend themselves to an amalgam of the old and the new; yet both also offer "new wine" that will inevitably burst old wineskins even as they are faithful to the Yahweh and Jesus of Scripture. The new wine of the kin-dom appears when the old and the new are blended by wise stewards who are openhearted in the face of necessary losses yet faithfully imaginative about possible worlds.[3]

If I read our times rightly, then I must also believe that God is indeed speaking in our times, as if "out of a burning bush" (Exod 3:2-4). Turning to Benedict, we notice that the Prologue to his Rule is filled with the idea of *call and response* (not law and punishment) as the primary metaphor for the spiritual life. Benedict emphasizes a concept of the spiritual life based on call as invitation: coaxing rather than demanding. He envisions an invitation that will require discipline, but not rigidity in response.[4] In a parallel way, Irish philosopher and public intellectual Richard Kearney offers an appealing example of God's call, taken from what he names "the inaugural moments of (Christian) faith," those involving Mary of Nazareth, the "Nazarena."[5] Kearney imagines that at the moment the angel Gabriel (the "stranger") appears, Mary is reading the narratives of her Abrahamic faith, with its stories of divine summons. Reliving the common past as she makes her leap of faith into the future, Mary is "freely choosing to believe that the impossible can be possible, that she can conceive a child. . . . She chooses."

From yet another perspective, one of the psalms Benedict appoints for reading every day includes this question, posed by the quarreling Hebrews as they trudged wearily through the desert (Exod 17:1-7; Ps 95:8), "Is God among us or not?" Rather than repressing doubt, Benedict reminds his readers that every day, each of us is summoned to this question, this doubt. Each day we must answer anew: Authentic questioning is natural, but when we first remind ourselves each day of the tradition we inherit, we also remind ourselves to listen with our hearts for God's initiating and continuing call to us. Benedict is consistent in his view that God's daily call is not primarily about sin and forgiveness; rather, it is *a call that invites us into intimate relationship.* God seeks out each of us and yearns for intimacy with us. Our authentic response to God's call will include some discipline, but it proceeds via imagination and ultimately continues in joy. We must find ways to be open to the imaginative possibilities within impossibility if we are to hear and respond to God today.

Imaginative Possibilities

If you are "allergic" to philosophy, you may want to skip the next few paragraphs. However, folks like me need a bit more grounding in the reliability of imagination. Fortunately we are able to draw on the work of twentieth-century French philosopher Paul Ricoeur, who carefully explored how new meanings emerge in language. He looked especially at the multiple interpretative possibilities that potentially arise in metaphor and story. In doing so, he constructed a reliable philosophy of imagination for us.

In the West, the gradual movement toward scientific analysis carried along with it a disparaging of imagination as unreliable and generally unimportant. At the time Ricoeur began to explore a philosophy of the imagination, he admitted that it appeared to be "a field of ruins of literal predication and multiple theories." But Ricoeur was fascinated about the way metaphor and story bring new meanings into language. Metaphor is a linguistic device designed to convey the meaning of one thing by comparing it to what might at first seem quite different. For example, one might metaphorically say, "the snow blankets the ground." The snow both is and is not a blanket, but the comparison allows the hearer to consider the similarity (set within the difference) between the blanket on a bed bringing warmth and protection with the way snow covers and protects any seedlings until spring comes. A metaphor is always both true and untrue. However, the *effect* of metaphor is what Ricoeur calls "semantic shock that in turn causes the spark of a new meaning." Things or ideas that were remote now appear as related.[6]

In this sense, imagination is a productive process and not merely a reproductive one. It tells us something new, not merely rehashing something we already knew. Through this surplus of meaning, the metaphor provides an indirect reference to *potential realities* in the world. The spark of new meaning potentially redescribes the world and remakes reality. To some extent in our age, Western philosophy has been rooted in the worldview of the Enlightenment: confidence in reason applied by the knowing human subject. Yet even that view has been overwhelmed by the "masters of suspicion," that is, Freud, Marx, and Nietzsche, who all take the position that illusory meanings are presented *in order to hide deeper (and less noble) meanings.* The combination of these two points of view is largely responsible for the twentieth-century attempt to purge all symbol and myth (i.e., imagination) in order to free language and indeed life from ambiguity.[7]

Ricoeur agrees that the "archeological work" of uncovering the lies we humans tend to tell ourselves is essential. However, he insists that perspective is only the beginning of self-understanding for us as people and communities because the whole truth about us must also include the things we aspire to and believe in. While ambiguous discourse is philosophically messy, it is the only kind of discourse appropriate to describe the depth and richness of human experience. Human experience itself is messy, and if we seek meaning in language, interpretation must be able to account not only for past intentions, but also for the possibilities opened "in front of" the text or narrative of life itself.[8]

The potentially positive role of imagination in revealing God's desire for this earth suggests C. S. Lewis's metaphor of the desire for heaven. Lewis calls it the secret we cannot hide and cannot tell: we cannot tell it because it has never actually appeared in our experience, but we cannot hide it because our experience is constantly suggesting it. What is the point, Lewis asks, of remaining conscious of a desire that no natural happiness will satisfy? Is there any reason to suppose that reality offers any satisfaction to it? Giving up on straightforward prose, Lewis tells a metaphorical story: "A person's physical hunger does not prove that they will get any bread; they may die of starvation on a raft in the Atlantic. But surely someone's hunger does prove that one comes of a race which repairs its body by eating and inhabits a world where eatable substances exist." Likewise, he concludes, "my desire for Paradise does not prove that I personally shall enjoy it, but I think it a pretty good indication that such a thing exists and that some people will."[9]

However we envision God, I am convinced that our present hope to re-form America's currently de-forming policies, now as in ancient Egypt, depends upon the same primary resource Moses relied upon to bring the Hebrews out of slavery in Egypt—the utterly free God, present in human history and powerful in the ways God chooses.

Our Faithful Response: Soul-Making

Prophecy and Spiritual Formation

Recall that the prophet's vision is twofold: on the one hand, the prophet must be somewhat immune to the totalizing imperial consciousness. Nevertheless, he must have a keen perception of what is *actually happening* in his culture at present. On the other hand, the prophet is listening attentively to and for the word of God. In short, the prophet's eye is on the contemporary scene and her ear is inclined to God.[10] The prophet's understanding of the present moment, however, is focused less on any immediate crisis and more on a God-informed vision of a cultural crisis that is enduring and resilient, but which may still be somewhat invisible to the community at large. The prophet is a person who stands in the presence of God, not as a messenger but as a witness. "In (the prophet's) words, *the invisible God becomes audible.* . . . The greatness of the prophet lies not only in the ideas he expresses, but also in the moments he experienced. His word is a testimony to God's power and judgment, to God's justice and mercy."[11] In other words, the prophet reveals that the "issue" that is central to God's concern (and the prophet's) is more than a momentary kerfuffle but is fundamentally that of a widespread but utterly de-forming cultural consciousness.

I'm inclined to think that today, the prophetic voice may well be communal rather than entirely individual. God's word to be spoken to and in our world may burst forth from church and nonprofit groups, rather than exclusively from "a hero-type." Fortunately, there are many resources to guide us, since in our time we have a wonderful array of living and dead

Christian saints' letters and books in English and other contemporary languages. However, if we faithfully follow the rich
and long-trodden path as it applies to us, I believe we can learn
reasonably well to recognize when God's voice is speaking.
We can only do the best we can and keep listening, following
spiritual patterns laid out by many spiritual "parents," as well
as in "God's imagination."

At this point, you may be asking, how did we get to spiritual
discipline, spiritual formation? Most of the previous chapters
are very directly about public policy issues. Even if we are
willing to go along with the idea that God's call is an important
ingredient in the re-formation of our culture, we might have
expected that now we would turn to specific public policy
ways to change things! How can spirituality possibly have any
meaningful impact on "real-world" issues? The irony about
that question is that lived spirituality is the only thing that
ever has or ever will have meaningful positive impact on the
real world. We have seen all too clearly that violence, hierarchy,
dominance, and imperial behavior are not successful in creating significant transformative change. Things may look a little
better for a brief period, but the only long-term effect of oppressive behaviors is to create resentment, anger, resistance,
and/or passivity and numbness. Such things can never produce compassion, genuine companionship, and real cultural
transformation. Response to God's call is not about a quick
"okay" that fails to touch our hearts and actions but is rather
about an intentional ongoing commitment to our own transformation and to that of our society.

So what is spiritual formation or soul-making, and how do
we do it? One way to start is to re-read the Pauline epistles in
the New Testament, stopping every time we encounter the
phrase "in Christ," or "Christ in us." Paul actually uses the
phrase or its equivalent 164 times in his few epistles. Take some
time with what Paul is saying when he uses that phrase. I
understand it to mean a sense of sharing Christ's life, both
"Christ in us" and also "our life in Christ." The phrase refers

to the unfolding of Christ's own character in our lives today, where Christ is at work opening the present and future of our experience, an experience so intimate that it effectively unites us with the divine purpose for our lives. Whatever such intimacy also involves, it will involve movement toward God's intentions for what might be called Christian maturity in the practice of beloved community. Hence, it will inevitably also involve the cleansing of excessive pride and self-reference, and bringing to light what had been hidden (Mark 4:22-23). The process itself may not always be pleasant, but the result definitely will be filled with deep joy.

Spiritual formation is not the same as education, though it may initially include it. Education is normally about the acquisition of empirical knowledge, *aiming for mastery and control.* In contrast to that, spiritual formation is about the *experience of relationship with Mystery.* Christian spiritual life is lived in the conviction that relationship with the God-Mystery is not only possible but essential for a full human life.[12] When Jesus spoke of Abba, Father, he was expressing the conviction that his relationship with God was intimate and personal, and by teaching his disciples to begin prayer with the words, "Our Father/Abba," he extended the possibility—and the invitation—of personal intimacy with God to all.

Spiritual formation is not meant to suggest the uniform regularity of a military group but is rather intended to bring to mind a potter's shaping of a pot. Even the pot metaphor is inadequate, however, because spiritual formation necessarily includes the *response* of a person or group, as well as the invitation of God. Spiritual formation is intended to open a person to the astonishing love of God, learning to live in joy and transforming consciousness. "Knowledge of God cannot merely be a conceptual grasp of reality; spiritual experience is not passive, nor should we accept by hearsay the existence and activity of God. The invitation of faith is to personal experience."[13] Spiritual formation is a dynamic process in a progressive unfolding of the person God intends and enables an individual or group to be and become. "All people are called to discover the unique form God hopes to give their lives. Not only will we gradually discover the form our life is to take, but also we will allow our daily existence to be an ongoing answer to this call. The core self is not of one's own making; it is God's gift to me, not a gift that I have, but a gift that I am. I answer this call in ongoing self-formation by a life that offers to God a whole-hearted *yes*."[14]

Benedictine Spirituality and Lectio Divina

To explore spiritual formation further, we turn to Benedictine spirituality, and in particular, to *lectio divina*, divine reading. In an April 2021 speech, Benedictine sister Joan Chittister made the point that, during the fall of the Roman Empire, a time of cultural de-formation similar to ours, the model that eventually eroded imperial consciousness was Benedictine life.[15] That Benedictine challenge succeeded not by competing with imperial consciousness on its own domineering terms, but instead by creating a new lifestyle, the "civic virtue" described by Rowan Williams early in this book.

The sixth-century *Regula* or Rule of St. Benedict sets forth a lifelong program to improve self-understanding and to transform the heart, beginning with a Prologue full of eager verbs: listen, open eyes and ears, set out, yearn for life. The goal is to "run on the path of God's commandments, our hearts overflowing with the inexpressible delight of love" (RB Prol. 49). Yes, there will be "a little strictness in order to amend faults and to safeguard love" (RB Prol. 47). The Rule is a measuring stick, not a punishment but a guide.[16]

Benedictines persistently aspire toward God, even or especially in the face of struggle. Benedictine Cardinal Hume observes that the Benedictine Rule is written as if for a community where things *will* go wrong! For example, Benedict specifies that in communal prayer, the first psalm be said *slowly*, so that everyone will be present by the time the second psalm begins.

He requires that *two* hot dishes be prepared for the main meal of the day, because otherwise someone is sure to object if only one is prepared and they can't eat whatever that item is. We are not to be surprised when we fall short of perfection, nor when we "lose" an engagement for causes about which we care passionately. Instead, the Rule encourages us to be realistic that we are people in process, and God is moving in our midst in ways we cannot now see.

Although Benedict does not specifically use the term "spiritual formation" in his Rule, the goal he sets is fullness of life for all. He continually refers to God's call, as well as to our growing ability to respond in openness to personal transformation. He expects that if and as we follow specific daily and long-term patterns based on Scripture, God will transform both us as individuals and the world in which we live. Clearly, Benedict serves a powerful and loving God. Throughout his Rule, which was written to include recommendations by other monastics of his time, Benedict keeps adding "love" to what others have written. In the Prologue, he adds the adjective "dear" to the word "brothers" (v. 19), describes the usual establishment of a school for the Lord's service with the additional words "we hope to set down nothing harsh, nothing burdensome" (v. 46), and explains that if anything seems a bit strict, it is so not just for the amendment of vices but also "to safeguard love" (v. 47).

Lectio divina, one of the primary means of spiritual formation in Benedict's Rule, is a Latin term meaning "divine (or holy) reading." The term, even in Latin, has a twofold meaning, first and mainly about meditating on Scripture (the divine or holy matter), and second, about a way of "reading" many things, to take them slower and more deliberately, moving more and more deeply into the nature of what anything is.[17] Susan Muto, dean of the Epiphany Academy of Formative Spirituality, describes this as "a special kind of reading, the words of which are directed primarily to our inner spiritual selves, a reading that prompts transformation and orients our whole being toward the Divine."[18] Benedict's Rule recommends that monastics spend four hours a day in this practice but does not describe it, suggesting that at least by the sixth century, *lectio* was a common practice in spiritual life. *Lectio* is probably an offshoot of the long-established practice in Judaism called *haga* or *haggadah*, as suggested in the first psalm (v. 2) of the Hebrew Scriptures, "Blessed is the one who meditates on the Torah day and night," and perhaps even from the Greek Gospel of Luke, chapter 2, where we are twice told that Jesus' mother Mary *ponders* unusual events. Both terms, "meditate" and "ponder," suggest a process that is not only mental, but also imaginative and something that evokes deep resonance and desire to respond.

The Christian monastic format for practicing *lectio* is attributed to the twelfth-century Carthusian, Guigo II. Guigo writes,

> I seek by reading and meditating what is true purity of heart and how it may be had, so that with its help I may know you, Lord, if only a little. . . . So give me, Lord, some pledge of what I hope to inherit, at least one drop of heavenly rain with which to refresh my thirst, for I am on fire with love. . . . The Lord, whose eyes are upon the just and whose ears can catch not only the words, but the very meaning of their prayers, does not wait until the longing soul has said all its say, but breaks in upon the middle of its prayer, runs to meet it in all haste and restores the weary soul.[19]

Classically, the steps that Guigo recommends are (1) reading, (2) meditating, (3) praying, and (4) contemplating. Unfortunately, most of those terms have taken on multiple meanings throughout time and space, so it is somewhat uncertain what they actually meant. For group practice of *lectio divina*, I have adopted the contemporary language of (1) hearing, (2) being touched, (3) asking for direction, and finally (4) waiting/praying.[20]

Carl McColman, lay associate of the Cistercian Monastery of the Holy Spirit, writes thoughtfully, "The key to lectio is not just in learning a four-step process, but also in rethinking your entire approach to the meaning and purpose of written words and how we use them. Lectio does not change the Bible, but it does change how we approach it. . . . When you practice lectio, you do not seek to control, but rather to yield. . . . Lectio divina involves opening your heart and soul in order to be formed (and transformed) by the Spirit of God."[21] Personal *lectio divina* has also been described as "the vibrant heart of Benedictine *conversatio*,"[22] that ongoing daily conversion of heart emphasized in the previous chapter. Other common Christian practices of spiritual formation include centering prayer, contemplation, and the like, each of which may be of value at different times in life, and/or to persons of differing temperaments. The keys are regularity in practice and the desire for God (which is already in our hearts due to God's initiative!).

Formative Participation in Community Life

Now again, you may be wondering something like, spiritual formation is obviously good for ongoing Christian life, but tell us again about how or why it might influence public policy? Is our role as a citizen not quite separate from our deepening life of faith? The Benedictine disciplines are designed to help us become free for God. And those disciplines pertaining to community are designed to help us become free of those ego impulses that routinely prevent wholehearted and effective engagement with others. Purity of heart is of value in *all* communal life, from the intimacy of family life to the bright light of public life.

In order to be effective in public policy discussions, we must be aware that human groups inevitably include people holding many diverse views. All of us carry traditional views of complexity and depth that we seek to have respected, even as we seek to respect others. On the other hand, none of us are exempt from self-interest, inflated egos, and certain blindnesses that tend to show up in such conversations. Although the purpose of spiritual formation remains centered in mutual construction of a strengthened relationship with the holy, it also necessarily involves the gradual freeing of each individual human heart from domination by our instincts. We may imagine that our forebears in faith understood far less than we do about what may today be called psychological issues and/or the numbness caused by imperial consciousness. Yet we need only read the work of Benedict's teachers, Evagrius and Cassian, to see how astute they were about the problem they called *apatheia* (the opposite of purity of heart), and what we might simply call distorted capacities for love.[23] The next paragraphs on community life offer more details about how Benedictine spiritual formation in community creates not only awe and trust in God, but also enables the casting away of the many delusions our egos so cherish, as well as help us gain insight into the ways imperial consciousness has de-formed our beliefs and opinions. Those delusions and that blindness not only create problems in personal relationships but also make us ineffective in public life.[24]

The task of prophetic imagination is immensely strengthened by the processes of soul-making as set forth in prophecy and in Benedictine spirituality. Both emphasize regular practices to help us hear and respond to God's call in the present moment. Specifically, the Benedictine practices of *conversatio* and *lectio divina* offer means for growth in nearness to God and create readiness to respond fully. The third Benedictine practice that forms our souls and spirits, participation in community life, is sometimes neglected when speaking to laity because the common life cannot provide quite the same opportunities, nor elicit the same demands, that monasticism finds central. Yet the "discipline of community" is essential even for non-monks to attain the spiritual formation we seek.

So what is the practice of community and how do we practice it outside of a monastery? Benedict's Rule—in contrast to other monastic rules of his time, which tended to regard the solitude of hermits as the most mature form of monastic life—calls those who live in community "the strong kind" (RB 1.13). Although monasteries tend to focus on enclosure or some form of withdrawal from the world, Benedict understood that novices will, in fact, bring "the world" with them as they enter. In the Rule, *community itself is a form of spiritual discipline* because in personal interactions, monastics are forced to face their "character defects," just as we are, who live the common life. As examples of Benedict's concern, his Rule insists that seniority is to be determined *only* by date of entry (making sure that wealthy or titled entrants were treated no differently than poor ones, or even immigrant "barbarians"), that competition is to be permitted only in showing respect to others, and that common tasks (like washing dishes) are to be shared by everyone. The Rule also contains a thoughtful section on punishments for offenses, of which the most severe is exclusion from community life. In specifying these things, Benedict encourages monastics to be attentive to the fact that potential moments of conflict in community are opportunities to grow in grace, to listen for God especially in times when we might feel offended or angry or dismissed, and to seek God in others when we need support or encouragement.

Benedict's guidance about community helps prepare those of us who live in the world for the work of public challenge. Just as other elements of spiritual formation help us witness the world more clearly, community life can help us not only understand what is true but also find the courage together to challenge our world more effectively and faithfully. Charles Mathewes, a professor of religious studies at the University of Virginia, proposes a theology of public life, suggesting that one reason for people of faith to engage in public life is to discipline our own dispositions, because participating in public life is actually a form of spiritual formation. Not unlike Benedict's valuing of community as sometimes a source of tension and dissatisfaction which, with the right disposition, can be turned into a call for God's help, Mathewes regards public life, resistant as it is to change, as calling forth the disposition of endurance that only intimacy with God can give.[25] As Christians we endeavor to realize the kin-dom of God[26] in humble openness to potential reconciliation with others, vulnerable to the possibility of change in ways their presence may elicit in us.[27]

Engagement with others for Christians is actually central to our personal response to God. In somewhat different language, Rowan Williams, previously archbishop of the Anglican communion, observes that "each member of the community regards relation with the others as the material of their own sanctification."[28] In other words, something about the Christian faith insists that we will not become fully holy as individuals, but only in the context of the church as the Body of Christ. In his earthly life, Jesus spent most of his ministry *with* others, and was known as one who even shared meals with "riffraff." St. Paul returns again and again to the metaphor of the Body of Christ. And several contemporary theologians regard the fact of the Trinity as expressing the reality that the essence of God's own inner life is communal.[29] Richard Rohr calls God "absolute relatedness," not only in God's own life as Trinity, but also inevitably pouring forth Godself into the humans God so loves. Therefore "we humans are intrinsically like the Trinity, living in an absolute relatedness, which we call *love.*"[30] Central to the life of Christians is the notion that we belong not only to God, but also belong to one another through Christ's love. This is the foundation of the Christian ideal of community and the reason it is so important in Benedictine life. Yet, despite this theological grounding, community is a seldom-experienced ideal, especially in the United States, which so values individual freedom.

Michael Casey, for sixty years an Australian Cistercian monk, in 2021 published a book on monastic community called *Coenobium*, "a Latin word derived from the Greek *koinos bios*, meaning 'the common life.' "[31] Casey urges us to recognize that "to have stepped over the threshold of the spiritual world . . . is to have a new vision of reality."[32]

Community life, as so much in Christian life, is a paradox. The early desert monastics viewed community as an opportunity for service and help to others. Indeed, the classic query to those who preferred the life of a hermit is, "Whose feet will you wash?" Sometimes, a reminder is offered of the model of mutual generosity in the Acts of the Apostles 4:32. Certainly such charity was not effortless but was the unfolding of mutual care tested in the light of serious challenges and supported in God's strength. Sometimes we turn to members of community for care and comfort, especially in light of a grievous loss or other sorrow. And yet, community life can also be a source of bracing challenge, reminding us to widen our viewpoint, to stand in solidarity with those left out. Prayer and Bible study are often strengthened in communal practice, though community liturgies should be supplemented with private prayer and reading.

The aim of Benedictine disciplines is to enable us, as individuals and community, to live into the fullness of life and the joy of wholeness that comes with awareness of the love of Christ. Yet of course, it remains true that the failures of love caused by the inherent self-centeredness of human beings (you and me included!) can make it difficult to live into Christ's promise. We must develop a way to understand genuine community as the product of conflict and testing. We must discover ways to be authentically present to and respectful of one another while we disagree strenuously. We must learn to discover and speak our own truths, without fear and without harm to others who also hold a piece of the truth in which we all live. Finally, we must be willing to acknowledge that no one of us has all the truth; my "opponent" may carry a portion of the truth to which I am blind. All those issues may be some of the reasons why the practice of community is so difficult.

Indeed, monastic writers often speak first of the many challenges involved in communal living. Reviewing some of the difficulties of community life mentioned by monastics may make it somewhat more explicit how this monastic practice is relevant to our participation in public life. Michael Casey mentions three vices that are primary obstacles to participation in community, public or private. Casey calls them by their monastic Latin names: *singularitas, cupiditas,* and *curiositas.*[33] Singularity roughly corresponds to individualism, cupidity to "a multiplicity of desires for temporal benefits" (perhaps boredom creating consumerism?), and curiosity meaning something like vanity, or focusing a great deal of attention on insubstantial things. Given the importance of individualism in America today, I'll further offer the list Casey includes of the practical effects of *singularitas,* which is to say, the way that particular vice (individualism) usually impacts community life:

1. We are unfeeling and uncompassionate about others' sufferings,

2. we have no interest in the common good,

3. we have a tendency to construct our own glory on others' ruin,

4. we desire to leapfrog others in our eagerness to get ahead,

5. we constantly affirm our superiority over others, and

6. we are more concerned with appearances than with reality.[34]

Casey observes that, given this list, it is no wonder that singularity and unhappiness are often associated. What I find so heartening, however, is Casey's observation that "mostly all it takes is the persevering practice of the everyday virtues that Pope Francis recommends: politeness, good humor, helpfulness, and forgiveness."[35] Some time ago, I realized that it is unrealistic to expect that all my family and friends think the same way I do, and it may help if I commit myself to a practice of kindness. Certainly, kindness is not up there with the great virtues, but it does make a considerable difference in building a loving community of mutual care. It is clear that life in the world, public life, even for Benedictine oblates and others who follow the Rule, will not have the same spiritual quality found in a monastery of consecrated women and men. Nevertheless, it is also true that when public engagement is undertaken in cooperation with the church, its guidance, and its members, and is coupled with some form of community discipline, public life too can be considered as participation in the mystery that is the sacred. Sometimes we think of prayer as a process only of intercession for others and/or petition, asking for our own needs. But the quality of prayer implicit in prophetic and Benedictine disciplines has to do most with waiting in silence for God to speak to us. My sense of God speaking to me comes less in the form of the actual hearing of a (human) voice than of a thought coming into my head that is a complete surprise, or something I've never considered before (and it may not come exactly in the prayer time but might surface later on when I'm not really thinking about anything).

Spiritual Formation and Denial

Sometimes it is tough to live with a particular problem and/or even to deal with something we might feel God is asking us to address, and that is where ongoing spiritual formation comes in. In chapter 2, regarding potential "wake-up calls" American culture has received and ignored in recent years, the psychological mechanism of denial was introduced. In our contemporary world, denial is an unconscious strategy most of us use occasionally. Denial can be a defense mechanism in which unpleasant thoughts, feelings, wishes, or events are ignored or excluded from consciousness. It may take such forms as a refusal to acknowledge the reality of a terminal illness, a financial problem, an addiction, or a partner's infidelity.[36] And denial can be a community strategy as well as a personal one, as we saw in America's cultural response to the 9/11 attacks and the COVID-19 pandemic.

Many situations and feelings can evoke denial, but it becomes particularly evident when we are confronted with something that feels threatening to us, for whatever reason. Initially, denial actually may be healthy if we need time to process something truly shocking, such as the sudden death of a family member or close friend. However, when faced with a real matter forcing us to deal with it directly, but we continually refuse to accept the reality, denial can be dangerous both on an individual level and a cultural one. Denialism is an essentially irrational action that withholds the validation of an historical experience or event, when a person refuses to accept an empirically verifiable reality. Examples of that danger might be when:

> Someone periodically misses morning work meetings after drinking excessively the night before, but insists there's no problem because the work is getting done;
> A couple are ringing up so much credit card debt that they toss the bills aside because they can't bear to open them; or
> The parents of a teen with drug addiction keep giving their child "clothing" money.

But it's important to realize that denial should only be a temporary measure—it won't change the reality of the situation. And it isn't always easy to tell if denial is holding you back. This is especially difficult when, as Richard Rohr observes in his book on addiction, "There are shared and agreed-upon additions in every culture and institution, . . . which are hardest to heal because they do not look like addictions because we have all agreed to be compulsive about the same things and blind to the same problems."[37] And given the difficulty of breaking the totalism of the American empire, it will likely be especially difficult to break through our cultural denial of the four de-forming issues set forth in section II of this book. Denial is the issue that will bring us to our knees in the face of these urgent problems. And they *are* urgent! That is why we so desperately need God and community support to address these de-forming issues now.

Let us consider two that will not wait long before collapse is upon us. In general today, we Americans have taught ourselves stories about our nation that are not precisely true. As we saw recently in the Glasgow Climate Summit (Cop26), after no less than thirty years of earnest appeals about human-forced climate change, our spokespersons and our governments are still talking but not investing significant resources into remedies. The situation has grown so stark that hundreds of species of plants and animals no longer live on our planet; it is not impossible that the human race will be the next to die off. Only a moral crisis (and dare I say, a spiritually based communal response) can now prevent that.

Also, I will speak of the urgency of attention to diversity and race. It is time that we face the outright lies with which America is comforting itself about race. *The Christian Century* published a cover story about theologian Willie Jennings's views on the place of race.[38] Jennings explains, "Inside the modern racial consciousness there is a Christian architecture, and there is also a racial architecture inside of modern Christian existence." While Christianity is "inside" Israel's story, early on the Gentiles began to "push Israel out from its own story." In doing so, Christians have distorted the older story, in order to claim that they/we "are at the very center of what God wants to do in the world." This form of the story hardens so that Whiteness takes on "the power not only to transform the land, but also to *shape the perceptions of themselves and others. . . .* Whiteness is a way of perceiving the world and organizing and ordering the world by the perception of one's distorted place in it."[39] Again here we encounter a statement/ story (as we did previously in the chapter on diversity) that at first seems so outrageous as to seem unbelievable, only to find it is a story being played out on the front pages of our daily newspapers and television screens about the teaching of race in public schools. Confronting the possibility that White children may feel shame if and when they learn the truth about systemic racism in America since the days of our founding, many American parents seem to feel that the actual history of our country should never be taught.

Systemic racism means that racism, or refusal of diversity as I have called it, was built into the fabric of our theoretically openhanded democratic institutions, and it remains there today. Systemic racism does not refer to how any one White American thinks of or treats people of color, but rather addresses the reality that many American institutions and policies still bear structures today that disadvantage people of color, and we must work together to change those institutions and policies. Systemic racism is not a statement about who an individual person's friends are, nor about the personal behavior of anyone whose skin is White, Black, Brown, Yellow, or Red. It is a simple and accurate statement about facts, such as that initially our US Constitution allowed no woman nor American Indian to vote, and only counted three-fifths of an American Black person in census information that determined how many congressional representatives any state might have. It is a simple and accurate statement that many southern US states did not erect statues of Confederate heroes until one hundred years after they had lost the Civil War, which in fact was a treasonous war against a democratically elected US government. It is finally a simple and accurate statement that individual Black people alive in 2021 had grandparents who were enslaved. And that is only to touch the surface of US historical racism.

Systemic racism is about US cultural and institutional practices that continue to affect individual lives. Yes, things are better now, and yes, many White Americans today genuinely endeavor to be openhearted to people of color and vice versa. Furthermore, people of all colors being what they are, many people of all colors will continue to be meanspirited and hateful, in contrast to the goals of formation in Benedict's Rule. But the call to awareness of systemic racism is to put all of us Americans now on notice that essential changes to our institutions are needed, as well as to invite us to be mutually respectful. Even though mutual respect does and will vary among cultures, nonetheless each one of us is today urged, even begged, to follow the basic principle of caring for one's neighbor, near and far, both in law and in day-to-day actions. Willie James opines in his book, *After Whiteness: Education in Belonging*, that only when we American people of all faiths know the wholeness of our own stories and understand that we all have been brought "inside" into a place of love and belonging by grace rather than solely by right, only then will we find our way to mutual and ongoing fullness of life.[40] Profound gratitude should be offered to those who are assisting all of us to recognize these truths, as well as profound respect to those who still are culturally blind. Each of us finds our own way, but in time, the possibility of reconciliation may erode away.

Participation in Community

This seems a good point to return to the community's helpfulness in enabling us to face truth, in the context of a community guided by love and full of mutual care. I believe that one of the reasons for the rapid growth today in the number of oblates and others who retreat to monasteries and eagerly read Benedictine books is that we see how Benedict and his followers learned to turn creative conflict into genuine peacemaking. When we take seriously the call to transform ourselves and the world into the kin-dom of God, we see our work as Christians to be bringing transformation into the broken places of the world. We are able to stay lovingly in the world, always on the lookout for Christ within it, as we persist in inviting Christ to be manifest wherever discord or suffering exist. Returning to the reflections of Rowan Williams as we began this book, it is relevant to include Williams's observation that "Benedictinism is a model of active Christian life in itself; the vision of human possibility and dignity contained in Benedictine witness is a sketch of political virtue." Williams adds that Benedict did not invent these political virtues. "It could rightly be said that the Rule is simply a concrete example of the politics of the Body of Christ, emphasizing (1) the centrality of mutual service, (2) attention to the distinctive gift of each to all, and (3) above all the conviction that we are made for contemplative joy."[41]

In his book *Blessed Simplicity*, Raimundo Panikkar, a Roman Catholic theologian whose embrace of Hindu scriptures and Buddhism made him an influential voice for promoting dialogue among the world's religions, considers a useful approach to the present conflicting aims in our world to seek a new harmonious complexity. Panikkar speaks of the modern monk's desire to *transform* all things in what he calls a "mysticism of integration." Acknowledging the problems raised both by blessed simplicity (renunciation of the world) and by harmonious complexity (transformation of the world), he nonetheless speaks to a vision of the kin-dom of God not situated in a transcendent heaven but found in a synthesis of all possible values. The world is not simple, so complexity must be met on its own terms. But it can potentially be transformed into harmony through consecration and offering to God.[42]

Interestingly enough, modern physics also gives us a hint of how to belong creatively to community. Physicist David Bohm first wrote a book on physics, calling it, *Wholeness and the Implicate Order*. Continuing to ponder these physical mysteries, Bohm began then wrote another book, *On Dialogue*, exploring possibilities for working with "the implicate order" in human communication, a method for use in groups at a deep level, allowing conflict to surface and become something altogether new. I imagine Bohm might call the underlying movement in dialogue "the implicate order," but I don't imagine he would object to our calling it "the Holy Spirit" or "God."

Bohm suggests that when we use this method of conversation, we are learning to "think together," as we practice seeking a variety of perceptions, insights, and observations, holding them dynamically together without defending or eliminating anything. At some point, a creative newness, constituted specifically by the particularities raised, will become evident.[43] This "dialogue" requires a considerable degree of attention, keeping track of the subtle implications of one's own assumptions and reactive tendencies, while also sensing similar patterns in the group as a whole. "Dialogue" also requires a relaxed, nonjudgmental curiosity to see things as freshly and clearly as possible. Each participant revisits what he or she knows, realizing that it is not just other persons we encounter in dialogue, but also the living God. We need one another to complete our vision so that it corresponds to God's vision.

Community completes the primary help that prophetic and Benedictine spiritual disciplines offer in challenge to deformation in American culture today. But we are also specifically speaking of *participation* in community. The term "participation" essentially refers to the reality that many religions begin with: the notion that we all belong to each other, that we exist in a world that is united, though importantly diverse, united nonetheless in some mysterious way such that the cells of all our bodies are made up of the dust of the first stars. And "we" here means everything, not only all humans, but plants and animals and minerals, the planet Earth itself. And that unity in diversity somehow finds its source in God, however understood.

Reflection on the deeper meaning of participation closes this book, pointing out again how our human efforts, guided and grounded in spiritual practice and community, need yet another component to undertake the work of renewal: the call and power of God to transform all we know. The linguistic root of the word "participation" is the Indo-European *kap-yo* which means taking, seizing, or catching.[44] How might that suggest participation? A hint is provided by philosopher and academic William Franke in his discussion of the evolving interpretive theory about the Bible. In his words, interpretation of the Biblical text begins to sound remarkably like *lectio divina*, "It is indeed 'the Word' rather than the words (which interpreters encounter), but since interpreters are in the embarrassing position of being unable to lay hold of that Word (because it expresses something beyond the culture in which it was written), they can only permit it to lay hold of them."[45] American theologian and philosopher David Tracy adds that classic texts (like the Bible and Dante's *Divine Comedy*) "make a claim that transcends any preunderstanding I try to impose on them, a claim that can shock me with insight into my finitude as finitude, *a claim that will interpret me* even as I struggle to interpret it. I cannot control the experience. . . . It happens, it demands, it provokes."[46]

The root word forming participation suggests that the interaction between text and interpreter is not primarily a matter of human choice, as it is fundamentally about *being grasped by something central to the nature of reality*. In this section, I encourage you, dear reader, to expand your notion of empirical cause and effect in the light of what could be called soul-making. Even physicist Albert Einstein leads us to consider something like soul-making in a note he sent to a grieving father whose young son had just died of polio. Einstein wrote, "A human being is a part of the whole called by us 'the Universe,' a part limited in time and space. We experience ourselves, our thoughts and feelings, as something separated from the rest—a kind of optical delusion of our consciousness. This delusion is a kind of prison for us, restricting us to our personal desires and to affection for a few persons nearest to us. Our task must be to free ourselves from this prison by widening our circles of compassion to embrace all living creatures and the whole of nature in its beauty."[47] Participation invites us to widen our view of what is possible within this universe we share.

Twentieth-century Swiss theologian and contemplative Hans Urs von Balthasar offers further insight into the process of participation in terms that ring with joy:

In theology there are no "bare facts" which, in the name of an alleged objectivity of detachment, disinterestedness and impartiality, one could establish like any other worldly facts, without oneself being (both objectively and subjectively) *grasped, so as to participate in the divine nature.* For the object with which we are concerned is human participation in God. . . . The double and reciprocal *ekstasis*—God's venturing forth to the human and the human venturing forth to God—constitutes the very content of dogmatics, which may then rightly be presented as a theory of rapture.[48]

Cultural historian Thomas Berry flatly states that "if we are ever to renew our sense of the sacred, . . . we must appreciate the universe beyond ourselves as a revelatory experience of that numinous presence whence all things come into being. We become sacred by our participation in this more sublime dimension of the world about us."[49] Renewal of our appreciation of the way we humans participate with one another, with God, and with all aspects of life in and on earth is essential in what lies ahead.

Let us respond to the initiative and invitation of God with love, disciplines of spiritual formation, joining in community, and a spirit of participation in and with all. Let God's love transform our hesitation and fear. Let us learn to listen deeply and attentively, in silence and also to the world around us. Let us continue to look for beauty and practice joy. Every day let us find gratitude and awe in what is given us.

Practice of Conscious Community*

1. Sit in a circle. After the facilitator's initial introduction of the process, there is no leader. The group is constituted as community, with mutual responsibility, and discovers its own way of proceeding.

2. There is no agenda. The community is not trying to accomplish any useful thing.

3. The intention is to notice and respond to a surrounding but invisible guidance. As assembled community, we are creating a space for the Spirit to enter and speak among us.

4. Each one is to make contact with the ideas in your heart. Imagine that your heart's knowledge is connected to the heart knowledge of everyone else present, through the Divine Heart. Breathe.

5. When an idea forms in you, speak it as clearly and simply as possible. Speak for yourself, from your experience. Talk directly to others across and around the circle.

---

*Physicist David Bohm theorized that the universe itself includes an "implicate order" that can be assessed by attentiveness to it. Subsequently, he wrote a book called *On Dialogue* outlining a process much like the above, as a means to engage the implicate order within human communications. A process like this has actually been used with business groups willing to experiment with deeper understanding. Also, Suzanne Farnham has written *Grounded in God: What is Enlightenment?* outlining a similar listening process designed to strengthen and ripen possibilities.

6. After each comment, allow at least thirty seconds to pass, allowing everyone to absorb what was said. Listen fully with your entire self (senses, feelings, intuitions, imagination, and rational faculties). Only then form your response.

7. Speak your opinion as seems appropriate, when relevant, *owning your own* strong feelings. Focus on the present moment (what comes up out of all this for you right now? Or, what's nudging you here?).

8. Allow your deep assumptions to arise. Then, suspend your assumptions, that is, neither believe nor disbelieve in them, but simply notice them. Do not judge yourself. Do not devalue another, even inwardly. Breathe.

9. Watch for patterns that surface, listening to what is said and not said. Explore your feeling tone and that of the community, noticing as emotions or body responses occur. Pay attention to the "felt sense" of what is going on.

10. Allow conflict to emerge naturally. If an emotional charge builds up, stay with it, respectfully. And keep watching: what happens then? What is the cost of holding a non-negotiable opinion?

11. In silence, be open to deeper responses arising in the community. What do you see in the mirror? Reflect over your initial responses and ask what other possibilities exist as ways of understanding the issue?

12. Be receptive to whatever else might be seeking entrance here. Breathe. Watch for the emergence of a participatory consciousness, when every person in the room is suspending, and all are looking at everything together, and freedom emerges for transformation.

13. Trust the process.

For Further Reading

Many notes are presented in the text itself. However, several books important to me take up a task similar to mine, that is, (1) an assessment of how the United States is doing today, along with recommendations for constructive change, or (2) emphasis on a resource we need to practice more widely. Some readers will already be familiar with these, as they have been published over the last twenty years. It is past time for deepened contemplation and action together. Those books are listed here.

Thomas Berry. *The Great Work: Our Way into the Future*. New York: Three Rivers Press, 1999.

Walter Brueggemann. *Mandate to Difference: An Invitation to the Contemporary Church*. Louisville, KY: Westminster John Knox Press, 2007.

Walter Brueggemann. *The Prophetic Imagination*. 40th Anniversary Edition. Minneapolis: Fortress Press, 2018.

John Dear. *Living Peace: A Spirituality of Contemplation and Action*. New York: Doubleday, 2001.

David C. Korten. *The Great Turning: From Empire to Earth Community*. Bloomfield, CT: Kumarian Press, 2006.

Ched Myers. *The Biblical Vision of Sabbath Economics*. Washington, DC: Church of the Savior, 2001. www.bcm-net.org.

Parker J. Palmer. *Healing the Heart of Democracy: The Courage to Create a Politics Worthy of the Human Spirit.* San Francisco: Jossey-Bass, 2011.

Rosemary Radford Ruether. *Integrating Ecofeminism, Globalization, and World Religions.* Lanham, MD: Rowman and Littlefield, 2005.

Cornell West. *Democracy Matters: Winning the Fight Against Imperialism.* New York: Penguin, 2005.

Notes

Preface

1. The essay originated in the second lecture of a series Weber gave in Munich to the Free Students Union of Bavaria on January 28, 1919, but it was not translated into English until after World War II. The lecture can be found at https://www2.southeastern.edu/Academics/Faculty/jbell/weber.pdf.

2. Several years ago the esteemed journal *The Economist* boasted a cover story and special report titled "The New Wars of Religion," calling religion "the opium of the people" that provokes a "clash between superstition and modernity," while suggesting that the twentieth century rightly banished religion from politics because progress required secularism! (My exclamation mark.) November 3, 2007, https://www.economist.com/special-report/2007/11/03/the-new-wars-of-religion.

3. For example, see Rod Dreher, *The Benedict Option: A Strategy for Christians in a Post-Christian Nation* (New York: Sentinel Books, 2017).

4. Timothy Fry, ed., *The Rule of Saint Benedict 1980* (Collegeville, MN: Liturgical Press, 1981). Quotations of the Rule are taken from this version.

5. The Rt. Rev. Rowan Williams, then Archbishop of Canterbury, in a speech on Benedict's Rule delivered in Rome at the Benedictine House of Studies, 2006, in chap. 5, "Benedict and the Future of Europe," in Rowan Williams, *The Way of St. Benedict* (New York: Bloomsbury Continuum, 2020).

Chapter 1

1. Richard Kearney, *Reimagining the Sacred* (New York: Columbia University Press, 2016), 261.

2. R. W. J. Austin, "Introduction," *Ibn al-'Arabi: The Bezels of Wisdom* (Mahwah, NJ: Paulist Press, 1980), 4.

3. Sr. Iona Misquitta, "Pilgrims in Dialogue," *First World Congress of Benedictine Oblates* (Rome: Incipit Imaging for Official Manuscript, September 19–25, 2005), 137.

4. Rudolph Otto, *The Idea of the Holy*, trans. John W. Harvey (New York: Oxford University Press, 1958 [1923]).

5. Otto, *Idea of the Holy*, 5.

6. Abraham Heschel, *The Prophets* (New York: Harper, 1962), 19.

7. Alex Tuckness, "Locke's Political Philosophy," in *The Stanford Encyclopedia of Philosophy*, https://plato.stanford.edu/archives/win2020/entries/locke-political/.

8. Robert Bellah, *The Robert Bellah Reader* (Durham: Duke University Press, 2006), 231, 259, 230.

9. According to the *Catechism of the Catholic Church*, there are two testaments to the Christian Bible that have been traditionally referred to as Old and New; hence the use of the term Old Testament is to be preserved as part of the common language and heritage of our faith. In that sense, many terms of Christian faith received their beginnings in the wisdom of the Hebrew heritage that we embrace. It is not to be understood that Christians have appropriated specific terms for our *exclusive* use, such as chosen people, received through our older heritage, although I apologize personally for any offense taken.

10. Bellah, *Robert Bellah Reader*, 127.

11. Bellah, 227–29.

12. Cornel West offers this reminder of past critiques of America in *Democracy Matters: Winning the Fight Against Imperialism* (New York: Penguin, 2004), 13.

13. See, for example, Hent de Vries and Lawrence E. Sullivan, eds., *Political Theologies: Public Religions in a Post-Secular World* (New York: Fordham University Press, 2006).

14. West, *Democracy Matters*, chap. 5, beginning on p. 146.

15. Walter Brueggemann, *The Prophetic Imagination*, 40th anniv. ed. (Minneapolis: Fortress Press, 2018), 21.

16. West, *Democracy Matters*, 13.

17. Benedict takes a passage from Matthew 13:52, to be repeated in the Rule, 64.9, "The Election of an Abbot": "He ought, therefore, to be learned in divine law, so that he has a treasury of knowledge from which he can *bring out what is new and what is old*" (emphasis original). For me, this passage centers us right where we Christians need to be, in these times.

18. Michel Philibert, "Philosophical Imagination: Paul Ricoeur as the Singer of Ruins," in *The Philosophy of Paul Ricoeur*, Library of Living Philosophers XXII, ed. Lewis Edwin Hahn (Chicago: Open Court, 1995), 128.

19. Maimonides was a medieval Jewish philosopher who was very influential in Jewish thought and philosophy in general. Maimonides is cited in Devon Anderson's article, "Church Needs Prophetic Action Plan," in the *Episcopal News Monthly*, November 20, 2010, p. 2.

20. Brueggemann, *Prophetic Imagination*, 111.

21. Heschel, *Prophets*, 25.

22. Heschel, 618.

23. Heschel, 291.

24. Walter Brueggemann, "How God Intervenes," *Sojourners*, January 2018, p. 21.

25. Brueggemann, *Prophetic Imagination*, xxix.

26. Brueggemann, 3.

27. In 2005, the Benedictine House of Studies in Rome, Italy, realized that there were about the same number of oblates worldwide as there were monastics—about 25,000 of each. An Oblate Congress was held in Rome that year—and every four years since—with oblates attending from all over the world, and every presentation translated into five languages. I am grateful to have attended as one of only six invited plenary speakers, and the only one from the US.

28. The Rt. Rev. Rowan Williams, 2006 presentation at the Benedictine House of Studies in Rome, Italy, in chap. 5, "Benedict and the Future of Europe," in Rowan Williams, *The Way of St. Benedict* (New York: Bloomsbury Continuum, 2020).

Chapter 2

1. Robert Bellah, "Can We Be Citizens of an Empire?," talk given at Iliff School of Theology, Denver, CO, January 28, 2003. A version of this talk was also delivered at Pepperdine University in Malibu, CA, on March 6, 2003, and an abbreviated version of it, entitled "Righteous Empire," was published in the March 8, 2003, issue of *The Christian Century*. See http://www.robertbellah.com/lectures_8.htm.

2. Bellah, "Can We Be Citizens?"

3. Bellah.

4. Ernest R. May, *Imperial Democracy: The Emergence of America as a Great Power* (New York: Harcourt, Brace, & World, 1961), 270.

5. Chalmers Johnson, *The Sorrows of Empire: Militarism, Secrecy, and the End of the Republic* (New York: Henry Holt, 2004), 2.

6. Andrew Bacevich, *American Empire: The Realities and Consequences of U.S. Diplomacy* (Cambridge: Harvard University Press, 2002), 127.

7. William Appleton Williams, *Tragedy of American Diplomacy* (New York: Norton, 1988).

8. Bacevich, *American Empire*, viii; and David Ray Griffin, John B. Cobb Jr., Richard Falk, and Catherine Keller, *The American Empire and the Commonwealth of God: A Political, Economic, Religious Statement* (Louisville, KY: Westminster John Knox Press, 2006), 7.

9. Joan Didion, "Fixed Opinions, or The Hinge of History," *New York Review*, January 16, 2003, https://www.nybooks.com/articles/2003/01/16/fixed-opinions-or-the-hinge-of-history/.

10. Tom Pyszczynski, Sheldon Solomon, and Jeff Greenberg, *In the Wake of 9/11: The Psychology of Terror* (Washington, DC: American Psychological Assn., 2003), 4.

11. Bellah, "Can We Be Citizens?"

12. John Cobb, "Imperialism in American Economic Policy," in Griffin et al., *American Empire*, 40, notes that "one of the necessities for an effective empire is the control of one's own people. . . . The events of 9/11 made national security the primary issue, and individual rights can be curtailed in the name of security. Much of what is in the USA PATRIOT Act (based on NS2002) is more directed to providing a context in which civil disobedience and protest can be controlled than to preventing foreign nationals from attacking us."

13. Griffin et al., *American Empire*, 12. See also https://georgewbush-whitehouse.archives.gov/nsc/nss/2002/.

14. Bellah, "Can We Be Citizens?" quotes directly from Bush's September 2002 National Security Document. See further details in the following paragraphs.

15. Griffin et al., *American Empire*, 12, 17.

16. General Howell M. Estes, "United States Space Command: Vision for 2020," 1997, https://thecommunity.com/vision-for-2020.

17. Griffin et al., *American Empire*, 13.

18. Tim Weiner, "Air Force Seeks Bush's Approval for Space Weapons Programs," *New York Times*, May 18, 2005, front page. For additional information, see George Friedman and Meredith Friedman, *The Future of War: Power, Technology, and American World Dominance in the 21st Century* (New York: St. Martin's Press, 1998).

19. John W. Dean, Book Review, "Liberties Disappearing Before Our Eyes," *Los Angeles Times*, September 21, 2003, https://www.latimes.com/archives/la-xpm-2003-sep-21-bk-dean21-story.html.

20. The same book review in the *Los Angeles Times* on Sunday, September 21, 2003, by John W. Dean observed: "As horrible as terrorism can be, it must be understood in context. Compared with the policy of mutually assured destruction of the Cold War (with its inherent potential of annihilating humankind), national security experts will tell you, privately, that terrorism's threat to Americans appears to fall somewhere between that of killer bees (which scare people but take very few lives) and drunken drivers (who frighten very few people while killing 17,000 annually)" ("Liberties Disappearing Before Our Eyes").

21. Judyth Hill, "Wage Peace," https://www.judythhill.com/wage-peace-poem. Used with permission.

22. Joan Chittister, "9/11, Five Years On," commentary, *Sojourners*, September/October 2006, https://sojo.net/magazine/septemberoctober-2006/911-five-years.

Claiming Your Voice

23. Wendell Berry, "Thoughts in the Presence of Fear," permanent archive, *Orion,* https://orionmagazine.org/article/thoughts-in-the -presence-of-fear/.

24. Reported in the *New England Journal of Medicine,* "First Case of 2019 Novel Coronavirus in the United States," March 5, 2020, https://www .nejm.org/doi/full/10.1056/NEJMoa2001191.

25. "WHO Director-General's Statement on IHR Emergency Commit- tee on Novel Coronavirus (2019-nCoV)," World Health Organization, January 30, 2020, https://www.who.int/director-general/speeches /detail/who-director-general-s-statement-on-ihr-emergency-committee -on-novel-coronavirus-(2019-ncov).

26. Joel Achenbach, William Wan, Karin Brulliard, and Chelsea Janes, "The Crisis That Shocked the World: America's Response to the Corona- virus," *Washington Post,* July 19, 2020, https://www.washingtonpost .com/health/2020/07/19/coronavirus-us-failure/.

27. Achenbach et al., "Crisis That Shocked."

28. Szu Ping Chan, "Coronavirus: 'World Faces Worst Recession since Great Depression,'" *BBC News,* April 14, 2020, https://www.bbc.com /news/business-52273988.

29. Randall Lane, "Greater Capitalism," *Forbes,* May 26, 2020, https:// www.forbes.com/sites/randalllane/2020/05/26/greater-capitalism -how-the-pandemic-is-permanently-reshaping-our-economic-system -for-the-better/.

30. Billionaire Robert Smith found out about the problem and created an electronic patch to make it work for small businesses, while involving the National Council of Black Churches, so that during the second tranche in May, 90,000 loans were processed to genuinely small and often minority-owned businesses; Lane, "Greater Capitalism."

31. Paul Waldman, "Opinion," *Washington Post,* April 29, 2020.

32. The editorial "Stolen Education" in *Christian Century,* July 29, 2020, reported that while the CARES Act specified that $127 million was to go to private schools, after the secretary's decision, the actual amount was $1.5 billion.

33. This data and that following in this paragraph appeared in Jim Wallis, "Reopening Will Require Truth, Unity, and Solidarity," *Sojourners,* April 23, 2020, https://sojo.net/articles/reopening-will-require-truth -unity-and-solidarity.

34. An immigration detention center in Farmville, VA, experienced more than 80 percent of its detainees testing positive for the virus, but only responded to a request for an outside medical expert after a district judge ruled they were required to do so. "Judge: Outside Experts Can Visit Immigrant Detention Center with Virus Outbreak," *Associated Press,* August 18, 2020, https://www.nbcwashington.com/news/local/judge

-outside-experts-can-visit-immigrant-detention-center-with-virus
-outbreak/.

35. Rakesh Kochhar, "Unemployment Rate Is Higher Than Officially Recorded, More So for Women and Certain Other Groups," Pew Research Center, June 30, 2020, https://www.pewresearch.org/fact-tank/2020 /06/30/unemployment-rate-is-higher-than-officially-recorded-more-so -for-women-and-certain-other-groups/.

36. Test Monki, "CREDO Donates to Groups Fighting Hunger on the Frontlines of the Coronavirus Pandemic," Credo Energy, May 18, 2020, https://www.credoenergy.com/2020/05/18/credo-donates-to-groups -fighting-hunger-on-the-frontlines-of-the-coronavirus-pandemic/.

37. Christopher Ingraham, "New Research Explores How Conservative Media Misinformation May Have Intensified the Severity of the Pandemic," *Washington Post*, June 25, 2020, https://www.washingtonpost .com/business/2020/06/25/fox-news-hannity-coronavirus-misinforma tion/.

38. Scottie Andrew, "America's Response to the Coronavirus Is the Most American Thing Ever," *CNN*, May 19, 2020, https://www.cnn.com/2020 /05/19/us/american-individualism-coronavirus-trnd/index.html.

39. Jack Healy and Dionne Searcey, "Two Crises Convulse a Nation," *New York Times*, May 31, 2020, https://www.nytimes.com/2020/05/31 /us/george-floyd-protests-coronavirus.html.

40. Brad Braxton, "Sad but Not Surprised," *Christian Century*, July 1, 2020, p. 27.

41. Rabbi Ted Falcon, Spiritual Directors International teleconference, March 21, 2020.

42. Rev. SeiFu Anil Singh-Molares, Buddhist priest and executive director of Spiritual Directors International, stated at the March 2020 teleconference.

43. Ernst Becker, *Denial of Death* (New York: Macmillan, 1973), ix.

44. Becker, *Denial of Death*, 26.

45. Becker, 58. This author notes that his phrase is a particularly interesting observation in light of the hoarding of toilet paper during the coronavirus months.

46. Pyszczynski et al., *In the Wake of 9/11*, 16.

47. The president and first lady recommended shopping! See Pyszczynski et al., 97.

48. Pyszczynski et al., 153.

49. Paul Ricoeur, "Memory and Forgetting," in *Questioning Ethics*, ed. Richard Kearney and Mark Dooley (New York: Routledge, 1999), 8–9.

50. Soong-Chan Rah, "How the Delusion of Exceptionalism Obstructs Lament," commentary, *Sojourners*, May 29, 2020, https://sojo.net/articles /how-delusion-exceptionalism-obstructs-lament.

Interlude A

1. Walter Brueggemann, *The Prophetic Imagination*, 40th anniv. ed. (Minneapolis: Fortress Press, 2018), 127.
2. Brueggemann, *Prophetic Imagination*, 7.
3. Brueggemann, 6.
4. Brueggemann, 6; emphasis original.
5. Brueggemann, 9.
6. Brueggemann, 45.
7. Brueggemann, 45, 64.
8. Brueggemann, 45.

Chapter 3

1. Alain Richard, *Roots of Violence in the U.S. Culture: A Diagnosis Towards Healing*, foreword by Richard Rohr (Nevada City, CA: Blue Dolphin, 1999), 43.
2. Dan Milmo, "The Woman Who Stood Up to Facebook," *The Guardian Weekly*, October 15, 2021, pp. 10–13.
3. Sheldon Wolin, "Postdemocracy," *Tocqueville Between Two Worlds* (Princeton, NJ: Princeton University Press, 2001), as cited in Cornel West, *Democracy Matters: Winning the Fight Against Imperialism* (New York: Penguin, 2004), 25.
4. John Cobb, in David Ray Griffin, John B. Cobb Jr., Richard A. Falk, and Catherine Keller, *The American Empire and the Commonwealth of God: A Political, Economic, Religious Statement* (Louisville, KY: Westminster John Knox Press, 2006), 23.
5. Rosemary R. Ruether, *Integrating Ecofeminism, Globalization, and World Religions* (Lanham, MD: Rowman and Littlefield, 2005), 34.
6. Ruether, *Integrating Ecofeminism*, 34–35.
7. Brueggemann, *Prophetic Imagination*, 131.
8. Richard, *Roots of Violence*, 43–46.
9. Wendell Berry, *What Are People For?*, separate chapter titled "What Are People For?" (Berkeley, CA: Counterpoint, 1990, 2010), 123–25.
10. Richard, *Roots of Violence*, 44–45.
11. Tex Sample, *Working Class Rage: A Field Guide to White Anger and Pain* (Nashville: Abingdon Press, 2018), 15.
12. David Leonhardt, "The American Dream: Quantified at Last," *New York Times*, December 8, 2016, and April 10, 2020. Based on research originally at Stanford University, later transferred to Opportunity Insights, a nonpartisan, not-for-profit organization based at Harvard University and directed by Raj Chetty, John Friedman, and Nathaniel Hendren; https://opportunityinsights.org/.
13. Leonhardt, "American Dream."

14. Sample, *Working Class Rage*, 26–28.

15. "Heads of Facebook, Amazon, Apple and Google Testify on Antitrust Law," *C-SPAN*, July 29, 2020, https://www.c-span.org/video /?474236-1/heads-facebook-amazon-apple-google-testify-antitrust -law#!.

16. Richard Gillette, here and in paragraph following, *The New Globalization* (Cleveland, OH: Pilgrim Press, 2005), 131.

17. Griffin et al., *American Empire*, 28.

18. Ruether, *Integrating Ecofeminism*, 4.

19. Griffin et al., *American Empire*, 29.

20. Ruether, *Integrating Ecofeminism*, 5.

21. Ruether, *Integrating Ecofeminism*, taken from Bruce Rich, *Mortgaging the Earth: The World Bank, Environmental Impoverishment and the Crisis of Development* (Boston: Beacon, 1994), esp. 49–106.

22. Griffin et al., *American Empire*, 31.

23. Griffin et al., 33.

24. Ruether, *Integrating Ecofeminism*, 5.

25. Griffin et al., *American Empire*, 34.

26. Ruether, *Integrating Ecofeminism*, 6.

27. *Pace e Bene* and other Catholic-based groups and individuals have been nonviolently protesting this "education" for several decades; https://paceebene.org/pace-e-bene-history.

28. Starhawk, *Webs of Power* (Gabriola, Canada: New Society Publishers, 2002), 21. Starhawk is the pen name of Miriam Siros, who has been an activist on behalf of the common good for many years, and has trained hundreds of people in active nonviolence, often risking her own life.

29. Starhawk, *Webs of Power*, 15. What follows is her story from notes made at the time.

30. Starhawk, 20.

31. Starhawk, 58.

32. Brueggemann, *Prophetic Imagination.*

33. Starhawk, *Webs of Power*, 113–14.

34. Pope Francis, "Amid the Crisis of Communal Commitment," The Joy of the Gospel (*Evangelii Gaudium*) 50–51.

35. Pope Francis, Joy of the Gospel 57; emphasis added.

36. Matthew Lau, "Opinion: Pope Francis Says Capitalism Causes Hunger," Toronto *Financial Post*, October 23, 2019, https://financialpost .com/opinion/opinion-pope-francis-says-capitalism-causes-hunger-this -isnt-the-first-time-hes-been-wrong-on-economics.

37. Ched Myers, *The Biblical Vision of Sabbath Economics* (Washington, DC: Church of the Savior, September 2001). For further information, contact: www.bcm-net.org.

38. Myers, *Biblical Vision*, 5–6.

Chapter 4

1. Richard W. Gillette, *The New Globalization: Reclaiming the Lost Ground of Our Christian Social Tradition*, foreword by Kenneth Leech (Cleveland, OH: Pilgrim Press, 2005), xv.

2. David Ray Griffin, John Cobb Jr., Richard A. Falk, and Catherine Keller, *The American Empire: A Political, Economic, Religious Statement* (Louisville, KY: Westminster John Knox Press, 2006), 3.

3. Griffin et al, *American Empire*, 137.

4. Thomas Berry, *The Great Work: Our Way into the Future* (New York: Three Rivers Press/Random House, 1999), 122.

5. These two paragraphs about American corporate history are summaries of chap. 11 in Thomas Berry's *Great Work*, 117ff.

6. David Leonhardt, "A Corporate Court," *New York Times*, October 19, 2020, https://www.nytimes.com/2020/10/19/briefing/amy-coney-barrett-voting-world-series-your-monday-briefing.html. Leonhardt was quoting American billionaire businessman Charles Koch in a 1974 speech, comparing the 1886 goals with corporate progress in the courts since then. As of April 2021, Koch was ranked as the 15th richest person in the world on the Bloomberg Billionaires Index, with an estimated net worth of $63.1 billion.

7. David C. Korten, *The Great Turning: From Empire to Earth Community* (San Francisco: Kumarian Press, 2006).

8. Luca Ventura, "World's Largest Companies 2019," *Global Finance* magazine, August 29, 2019.

9. Cornel West, *Democracy Matters: Winning the Fight Against Imperialism* (New York: Penguin, 2004), 59.

10. Vandana Shiva, *Who Really Feeds the World?: The Failures of Agribusiness and the Promise of Agroecology* (Berkeley, CA: North Atlantic Books, 2016), xvii.

11. Steve Lopez, "The Real Cost of That $8.63 Polo Shirt," *Los Angeles Times*, November 26, 2003.

12. Kenneth E. Boulding, *Three Faces of Power* (Newbury Park, CA: Sage, 1989), 10.

13. Chalmers Johnson, *Blowback: The Costs and Consequences of American Empire* (2000) and *The Sorrows of Empire: Militarism, Secrecy, and the End of the Republic* (2004; New York: Henry Holt).

14. Johnson, *Sorrows of Empire*, 3–4.

15. David Vine, professor of anthropology at American University and author of *Base Nation* in 2013, on the *TomDispatch* website, July 2012, https://tomdispatch.com/david-vine-u-s-empire-of-bases-grows/.

16. Editors, "Tax Dollars at Work," *Christian Century*, September 18, 2007.

17. Diego Lopes da Silva, Nan Tian, and Alexandra Marksteiner, "Trends in World Military Expenditure, 2020," Stockholm International Peace Research Institute, April 2021, https://sipri.org/sites/default/files/2021-04/fs_2104_milex_0.pdf.

18. The data and analysis in the immediately preceding paragraphs were researched and reported by *The Nation* magazine, September 14, 2020. Other sources confirm these approximate total military costs. Dan Grazier, of POGO.org (Project on Government Oversight), estimated that the real total for defense in 2020 was more than $1.21 trillion. Grazier, "How Bells, Whistles and Greed Blew Up the Defense Budget," https://www.pogo.org/analysis/2020/08/how-bells-whistles-greed-blew-up-the-defense-budget/. Also, Kimberly Amadeo of *The Balance* estimated a slightly lower total of $935 billion; https://www.thebalance.com/u-s-military-budget-components-challenges-growth-3306320.

19. "DOD Financial Management: Ongoing Challenges with Reconciling Navy and Marine Corps Fund Balance with Treasury" (GAO-12-132), retrieved January 2, 2012, with similar reports over a series of months and years.

20. David Alexander, "Lawmakers Skeptical of Cuts in 2013 Defense Budget," *Reuters*, February 15, 2012, https://www.reuters.com/article/us-usa-defense-panetta/lawmakers-skeptical-of-cuts-in-2013-defense-budget-idUSTRE81D20220120215.

21. Mandy Smithberger, "COVID-19 Means Good Times for the Pentagon," June 29, 2020, https://www.pogo.org/analysis/2020/06/covid-19-means-good-times-for-the-pentagon/.

22. Information in this paragraph was derived from Tom Engelhardt's "The Bermuda Triangle of National Security," April 3, 2014, https://tomdispatch.com/engelhardt-the-bermuda-triangle-of-national-security/.

23. "Conventional Arms Transfers to Developing Nations," chart in *Sojourners*, January 2008, p. 11.

24. Friends Committee on National Legislation newsletter, July/August 2020.

25. "Votes in Congress," Charlottesville *Daily Progress*, March 7, 2021, A7.

26. Joan Chittister, "Dear Bishops: Open Letter on the Morality of Nuclear Deterrence Addressed to the US Catholic Bishops," *Pax Christi* journal, August 4, 2008.

27. Jim Wallis, "A Call to Repentance," *Sojourners*, January 2008, pp. 13–14.

28. George Will, "History Not yet Repeated (Fingers Crossed)," *Washington Post*, August 6, 2020.

29. West, *Democracy Matters*, 5–6.

30. Ruby Sales, *Sojourners*, February 2021, p. 35.

Interlude B

1. As even the irascible Ben Franklin pledged on our behalf; see p. 11 of chapter 1.

2. *Bread and Justice* journal, issue 63, 3.

3. Walter Brueggemann, *The Prophetic Imagination*, 40th anniv. ed. (Minneapolis: Fortress Press, 2018), 66.

4. Václav Havel, *Disturbing the Peace: A Conversation with Karel Hvizdala*, trans. from the Czech and introduced by Paul Wilson (New York: Vintage Books, 1991).

5. Paul Ricoeur, *The Rule of Metaphor: Multi-Disciplinary Studies of the Creation of Meaning in Language*, trans. Robert Czerny, Kathleen McLaughlin, and John Costello, SJ (Buffalo: University of Toronto Press, 1977).

Chapter 5

1. Eucharistic Prayer C in the 2007 ed. of *American Episcopal Book of Common Prayer*, 370.

2. Kerry Emmanuel, *What We Know about Climate Change* (Cambridge, MA: MIT Press, 2007), 3.

3. Emmanuel, *What We Know*, 3.

4. Adapted from Rosemary R. Ruether, *Gaia and God: An Ecofeminist Theology of Earth Healing* (New York: HarperOne, 1989), 5, 40ff. For another fascinating summary of scientific cosmogony, see David C. Korten, *The Great Turning: From Empire to Earth Community* (Bloomfield, CT: Kumarian Press, 2006), 267ff.

5. Ruether, *Gaia and God*, 44–45.

6. Emmanuel, *What We Know*, 13.

7. "Climate Change Indicators in the United States," United States Environmental Protection Agency, https://www.epa.gov/climate-indicators.

8. Emmanuel, *What We Know*, especially 43–46.

9. The United Nations annually reports on the gap between goals and performance of various nation-states. The first of these, post the 2016 Paris Accords, begins with this statement of intentions; https://www.unep.org/resources/adaptation-gap-report-2018.

10. World Meteorological Organization, "New Climate Predictions Increase Likelihood of Temporarily Reaching 1.5 °C in Next 5 Years," May 27, 2021, https://public.wmo.int/en/media/press-release/new-climate-predictions-increase-likelihood-of-temporarily-reaching-15-%C2%B0c-next-5.

11. Fiona Harvey, "A Fragile Agreement: Inside the Final Hours of Cop26," Manchester *Guardian Weekly*, November 19, 2021, pp. 15–16.

12. David Wallace-Wells, *The Uninhabitable Earth* (New York: Tim Duggan Books, 2020), 10.

13. Wallace-Wells, *Uninhabitable Earth*, 39; emphasis added.

14. For example, the 2014 *Living Planet Report* documents that populations of vertebrate species have *declined by half* since 1970 (reported in World Wildlife Fund, *Living Planet Report 2014*, Gland, Switzerland).

15. Wallace-Wells, *Uninhabitable Earth*, 44.

16. World Bank, *Turn Down the Heat: Why a 4°C Warmer World Must Be Avoided* (Washington, DC: November 2012), 13.

17. Tom K. R. Matthews et al., "Communicating the Deadly Consequences of Global Warming for Human Heat Stress," *Proceedings of the National Academy of Sciences* 114, no. 15, April 2017.

18. Oriana Ramirez-Rubin et al., "An Epidemic of Chronic Kidney Disease in Central America: An Overview," *Journal of Epidemiology and Community Health* 67, no. 1, September 2012, 1–3.

19. Wallace-Wells, *Uninhabitable Earth*, 52.

20. Wallace-Wells, 66.

21. Wallace-Wells, 67–68.

22. Andrew Galbraith, "China Evacuates 127,000 People as Heavy Rains Lash Guangdong: Xinhua," *Reuters*, September 1, 2018, https://www.reuters.com/article/us-china-floods/china-evacuates-127000-people-as-heavy-rains-lash-guangdong-xinhua-idUSKCN1LH3BV.

23. Joan Didion, "Fire Season in Los Angeles," *The New Yorker*, August 27, 1989, https://www.newyorker.com/magazine/1989/09/04/joan-didion-letter-from-los-angeles-fire-season.

24. CalFire, "Top 20 Most Destructive California Wildfires," https://www.fire.ca.gov/media/t1rdhizr/top20_destruction.pdf.

25. Jason Horowitz, "As Greek Wildfire Closed In, a Desperate Dash Ended in Death," *New York Times*, July 24, 2018.

26. Rob Monroe, "How Much CO_2 Can the Oceans Take Up?," *Scripps Institution of Oceanography*, July 13, 2013. The reader is asked to note that the dates of some of these reports are almost a decade earlier. Obviously it takes a while for data to be collected and reported, so please consider that, given little effective mitigation in the intervening years, it is very likely that conditions have grown even more severe than reported here.

27. "Coral Reef Ecosystems," National Oceanic and Atmospheric Administration, www.noaa.gov/resource-collections/coral-ecosystems; and *Global Aquaculture Advancement Partnership Program*, The United Nations Food and Agriculture Organization Subcommittee on Aquaculture, October 7–11, 2013.

28. Peter Brannan, "A Foreboding Similarity in Today's Oceans and a 94-Million-Year-Old Catastrophe," *The Atlantic*, January 12, 2018; and

The Worldwatch Institute, *State of the World 2015: Confronting Hidden Threats to Sustainability* (Washington, DC: Island Press, 2015), 5.

29. Joseph Romm, *Climate Change: What Everyone Needs to Know* (New York: Oxford University Press, 2016), 113.

30. Anna Oudin et al., "Association Between Neighbourhood Air Pollution Concentrations and Dispensed Medication for Psychiatric Disorders in a Large Longitudinal Cohort of Swedish Children and Adolescents," *BMJ Open* 6, no. 6, June 2016; and Hong Chen et al., "Living Near Major Roads and the Incidence of Dementia, Parkinson's Disease, and Multiple Sclerosis: A Population-Based Cohort Study," *The Lancet* 389, no. 10070, February 2017.

31. "7 Million Premature Deaths Annually Linked to Air Pollution," press release, Geneva, World Health Organization, March 25, 2014, https://www.who.int/news/item/25-03-2014-7-million-premature -deaths-annually-linked-to-air-pollution.

32. Wallace-Wells, *Uninhabitable Earth*, 54.

33. Vandana Shiva, *Who Really Feeds the World?: The Failures of Agribusiness and the Promise of Agroecology* (Berkeley, CA: North Atlantic Books, 2016), 1.

34. Shiva, *Who Really Feeds*, 2.

35. Shiva, 2.

36. Shiva, 3. It is important that we hear Shiva's voice, for she is rightfully troubled, and she has advanced some highly practical solutions, which of course, are not comfortable to imperial consciousness.

37. Shiva, ix–x.

38. Shiva, 29, and noted in the bibliography of her book *The Violence of the Green Revolution* (Lexington, KY: University Press of Kentucky, 2016); also see Marie-Monique Robin, *Our Daily Poison: From Pesticides to Packaging: How Chemicals Have Contaminated the Food Chain*, trans. Allison Schein and Lara Vergnaud (New York: New Press, 2016).

39. Barbara Kingsolver (and family), *Animal, Vegetable, Miracle: A Year of Food Life* (New York: HarperCollins, 2007), 13.

40. Shiva, *Who Really Feeds*, x.

41. Shiva, xi.

42. "Hungry for Land: Small Farmers Feed the World with Less Than a Quarter of All Farmland," *Grain*, May 28, 2014, https://grain.org /article/entries/4929-hungry-for-land-small-farmers-feed-the-world -with-less-than-a-quarter-of-all-farmland.

43. Amory Lovins, in Vandana Shiva, *Earth Democracy: Justice, Sustainability, and Peace* (Berkeley, CA: North Atlantic Books, 2005).

44. Shiva, *Who Really Feeds*, xiii; emphasis added.

45. Shiva, 8.

46. Shiva, 15–16.

47. Shiva, 41–42.

48. Shiva, 53.

49. Shiva, 86.

50. Kingsolver, *Animal, Vegetable, Miracle*, 116.

51. Shiva, *Who Really Feeds*, 57.

52. As noted previously, please also see Wendell Berry, *What Are People For?* (Berkeley, CA: Counterpoint, 1990), 111: "In encouraging women and other family members to work *off* the farm, 'the abstract and extremely tentative value of money is thoughtlessly allowed to replace the particular and fundamental values of the lives of household and community.'"

53. Joel Dyer, *Harvest of Rage: Why Oklahoma City Is Only the Beginning* (Boulder, CO: Westview, 1998); and Vandana Shiva and Kunwar Jalees, *Seeds of Suicide* (New Delhi: Navdanya, 2006), 48.

54. Shiva, *Who Really Feeds*, 86.

55. Kingsolver, *Animal, Vegetable, Miracle*, 50.

56. Shiva, *Who Really Feeds*, 68–69.

57. Vandana Shiva, *Soil Not Oil: Climate Change, Peak Oil, and Food Security* (Cambridge, MA: South End Press, 2016), 97.

58. Kingsolver, *Animal, Vegetable, Miracle*, 5.

59. Shiva, *Who Really Feeds*, ix.

60. Worldwatch Institute, *Confronting Hidden Threats*.

61. Worldwatch Institute, 7.

62. Worldwatch Institute, 22.

63. Worldwatch Institute, 27; emphasis added.

64. Worldwatch Institute, 30.

65. Worldwatch Institute, 31.

66. Worldwatch Institute, 33.

67. Worldwatch Institute, 35.

68. "National Reality Disorder with Robert J. Lifton," *Opinion Today*, November 8, 2019, https://opiniontoday.com/2019/11/08/national-reality-disorder-with-robert-j-lifton.

69. Korten, *Great Turning*, 253ff.

70. Korten, 258.

71. Korten, 263.

72. Thomas Berry, *The Great Work: Our Way into the Future* (New York: Three Rivers Press, 1999), 104.

73. Ruether, *Gaia and God*, 5.

74. Ruether, 4.

75. Ruether, 47–48.

76. Pierre Teilhard de Chardin, *Hymn of the Universe* (New York: Harper and Row, 1965), 68–69.

Chapter 6

1. The ancient root word for mercy is "womb-love," love for one who is of my body.

2. Vandana Shiva, *Who Really Feeds the World?: The Failures of Agribusiness and the Promise of Agroecology* (Berkeley, CA: North Atlantic Books, 2016), xi.

3. Wendell Berry, *What Are People For?* (Berkeley, CA: Counterpoint, 2010), 109.

4. Berry, *What Are People For?*, 113.

5. Berry, 121.

6. Rosemary R. Ruether, *Gaia and God: An Ecofeminist Theology of Earth Healing* (New York: HarperOne, 1992), 2–3; emphasis added.

7. Ruether, *Gaia and God*, 5.

8. Berry, *What Are People For?*, 8.

9. Refer to Kenneth Boulding, *Three Faces of Power* (Newbury Park, CA: Sage, 1989), cited in chap. 4 above, p. 77.

10. David Ray Griffin, John B. Cobb Jr., Richard A. Falk, and Catherine Keller, *The American Empire and the Commonwealth of God: A Political, Economic, Religious Statement* (Louisville, KY: Westminster John Knox Press, 2006), 4.

11. Stephen Charleston, "The Cost of Lies," *Christian Century*, December 30, 2020, p. 34.

12. Griffin et al., *American Empire*, 4, 159.

13. Denny Ludwell, *America Conquers Britain: A Record of Economic War* (New York: Alfred A. Knopf, 1930).

14. Cornel West, *Race Matters*, 25th anniv. ed. (Boston: Beacon Press, 2017), 107.

15. West, *Race Matters*, 108.

16. Dawn Araujo-Hawkins, "Majority of White Christians See No Pattern in Killings," reporting on a June 2020 American Values Survey, *Christian Century*, pp. 14–15.

17. Mark Bowes, "Grand Jury Finds Police Action Justified," *Richmond Times Dispatch*, February 27, 2021; reprinted later in *The Daily Progress*, Charlottesville, VA. As with the "racial script" described above, the young man was foolish and potentially dangerous to other drivers. An altercation when police stopped him resulted in his being fatally shot by the police, who later pointed out that he had marijuana in his bloodstream and a pistol was found in his possession.

18. Joshua Dubler and Vincent W. Lloyd, "A World Without Prisons," *Sojourners*, December 2020, p. 29ff.; and West, *Race Matters*, x.

19. Sarah Schwartz, "Map: Where Critical Race Theory Is Under Attack," *Education Week*, June 11, 2021, https://www.edweek.org/policy-politics/map-where-critical-race-theory-is-under-attack/2021/06.

20. Jim Wallis, "Bad Theology, Not Sociology," *Sojourners*, December 10, 2020, https://sojo.net/articles/bad-theology-not-sociology.

21. Dr. Michael Williams, staff doctor at UVA Medical School, presentation at St. Paul's Memorial Church, Charlottesville, VA, March 14, 2021.

22. The Rev. Liz Theoharis, cochair of the Poor People's Campaign, "Food Lines in the Land of Plenty," *Sojourners*, March 2021, p. 24.

23. Dr. Reggie Williams, "The Racial Script," *Christian Century*, September 23, 2020, p. 22ff.

24. Williams, "Racial Script," 23.

25. Williams, 23.

26. Williams, 24.

27. Williams, 24.

28. Robin Lally, "Police Use of Fatal Force Identified as a Leading Cause of Death in Young Men," *Rutgers Today*, August 8, 2019, https://www.rutgers.edu/news/police-use-fatal-force-identified-leading-cause-death-young-men.

29. These early theories of race have long since been debunked, but by then, the White supremacy script was well rooted in American life and culture.

30. Williams, "Racial Script," 25.

31. Williams, 25.

32. Audre Lorde, *Sister Outsider, Essays and Speeches* (Freedom, CA: Crossing Press, 1984), 115.

33. Kelly Brown Douglas, "The Legacy of the *White Lion*: A Christian Case for Slavery Reparations," *Sojourners*, July 2020, pp. 22–27

34. Douglas, "Legacy of the *White Lion*," 25.

35. Douglas, 25.

36. West, *Race Matters*, xv.

37. West, xv.

38. West, vii.

39. Meryl Kornfield, Christopher Rowland, Lenny Bernstein, and Devlin Barrett, "Purdue Pharma Agrees to Plead Guilty to Federal Criminal Charges in Settlement over Opioid Crisis," *Washington Post*, October 21, 2020, https://www.washingtonpost.com/national-security/2020/10/21/purdue-pharma-charges/.

40. Kornfield et al., "Purdue Pharma."

41. Anne Case and Angus Deaton published *Deaths of Despair and the Future of Capitalism* (Princeton, NJ: Princeton University Press, 2020), in which they created the term "deaths of despair."

42. Jonathan Sacks, *The Dignity of Difference: How to Avoid the Clash of Civilizations* (London: Continuum, 2002), 76.

43. See chap. 1 and Interlude A earlier in this book for a review of Brueggemann's insights on forms of consciousness.

44. Ann Ulanov, presentation at the Trinity Institute on "The Other: Embracing Pluralism," January 25, 1994.

45. Ilhan Omar, "When I Spoke Out about Systemic Oppression, the Republican Response Was Vicious," Opinion, *Washington Post*, July 15, 2020, https://www.washingtonpost.com/opinions/ilhan-omar-when -i-spoke-out-about-systematic-oppression-the-republican-response-was -vicious/2020/07/15/.

46. Ulanov, "The Other" presentation.

Interlude C

1. Jean-Francois Lyotard, *The Postmodern Condition* (Minneapolis: University of Minnesota Press, 1984).

2. Patricia M. Y. Chang, "Puzzled by Pluralism," *Christian Century*, September 6, 2003, p. 8.

3. Walter Brueggemann, "God's Otherness and Our Othering," presentation at the Trinity Institute, Trinity Church, NY, on "The Other: Embracing Pluralism," January 25, 1994.

4. Brueggemann, "God's Otherness."

5. Robert Kegan, "Conflict, Leadership, and Knowledge Creation," in *Women's Spirituality*, ed. Joann Wolski Conn, 2nd ed. (New York: Paulist Press, 1986, 1996), 131ff.

6. Ishpriya Mataji, "No More Sea!," *The Way* journal, October 1995.

7. Robert W. Radtke, "Inhabiting a Liminal Space," *Seek & Serve*, Fall 2021 newsletter, President's Column, 2.

Chapter 7

1. Abraham J. Heschel, *The Prophets* (New York: Harper, 1962), 19.

2. C. S. Lewis, *The Weight of Glory* (New York: MacMillan, 1965), 56.

3. Lewis, *Weight of Glory*, 59.

4. Soong-Chan Rah, "Lament Is the Appropriate Response to the Reality of Pain," *Sojourners*, March 22, 2021, https://sojo.net/articles/lament -appropriate-response-reality-pain.

5. Both of these rather superficial options are in contrast to the reflective work of theologian Dorothee Soelle in her book *Suffering* (Minneapolis: Augsburg Fortress, 1984), cited in Jason A. Mahn, "The Bible and the Pandemic," *Christian Century*, October 21, 2020, p. 30.

6. This is quoted in Derek Flood, "Where Is God When We Hurt?," *Huffington Post*, October 22, 2011.

7. Walter Brueggemann, as quoted in Mahn, "Bible and the Pandemic," 31.

8. Mahn, "Bible and the Pandemic," 32.

9. Nahum Ward Lev, foreword to Brueggemann's book, *The Virus as a Summons to Faith* (Eugene, OR: Cascade Books, 2020), ix.

10. Kathleen O'Connor, *Lamentations and the Tears of the World* (Maryknoll, NY: Orbis Books, 2002), 83–84.

11. Total number of deaths from coronavirus (COVID-19) in the United States as of April 18, 2022, https://www.statista.com/statistics/1101932/coronavirus-covid19-cases-and-deaths-number-us-americans/.

12. President Biden's reflections spoken at a sunset moment of grieving silence on February 22, 2021, "Remarks on Remembering the 500,000 Americans Lost to COVID-19," https://www.govinfo.gov/content/pkg/DCPD-202100157/html/DCPD-202100157.htm.

13. Dietrich Bonhoeffer's statement while in a Nazi prison during World War II, quoted by Reggie Williams in *Christian Century*, December 2, 2020, p. 25.

14. Known simply as "Strange Fruit," the song was written in 1930 by a New York man, Abel Meeropol, after the lynching of two young Black men in Indiana. Billie Holiday made it famous. https://www.litcharts.com/poetry/abel-meeropol/strange-fruit.

15. Rob Muthiah, "Lament as Antiracism Work," *Christian Century*, January 27, 2021, pp. 30–31.

16. Joan D. Chittister, OSB, *Heart of Flesh: A Feminist Spirituality for Women and Men* (Grand Rapids, MI: Eerdmans, 1998), 142–43.

17. See RB Prologue 49: "As we progress in this way of life and in faith, we shall run on the path of God's commandments, our hearts overflowing with the inexpressible delight of love."

18. Raimundo Panikkar, *Blessed Simplicity: The Monk as Universal Archetype* (New York: Seabury Press, 1982), 14, 16, 40–41.

19. Walter Brueggemann, *Praying the Psalms* (Winona, MN: Saint Mary's Press, 1986), 20–23.

20. Richard Rohr, *Breathing Under Water: Spirituality and the Twelve Steps* (Cincinnati, OH: Franciscan Media, 2011), xv, 31.

21. Rohr, *Breathing Under Water*, xxiii.

22. Rohr, 121.

23. Rohr, 31.

24. Ishpriya Mataji, "No More Sea!," *The Way* journal, October 1995.

25. Debra Dean Murphy, "Reading Genesis in a Dying World," *Christian Century*, October 23, 2019, p. 51.

26. Dennis Patrick Slattery, "The End of an Era" (personal note to this author, January 3, 2009—Dr. Slattery was prescient!).

27. Rt. Rev. Diana Akiyama, "Some Major Institutions are Falling Apart" (personal note to this author, February 5, 2009—she was prescient too. And both Slattery and Akiyama are persons of deep prayer).

28. Ewert Cousins, *Christ of the 21st Century* (New York: Continuum, 1992, 1998).

29. Ishpriya Mataji, "No More Sea!"
30. Brueggemann, *Prophetic Imagination*, 88.
31. Otis Moss III, "How Will Christians Answer This Moment in History?," *Sojourners*, July 30, 2020, https://sojo.net/articles/federal-troops -portland-protests-black-lives-matter.

Chapter 8

1. Ishpriya Mataji, "No More Sea!," *The Way* journal, October 1995.
2. Walter Brueggemann, *Prophetic Imagination*, 40th anniv. ed. (Minneapolis: Fortress Press, 2018), 127.
3. Benedict's Rule uses a quote from Matthew 13:52 in 64.9, on "The Election of an Abbot": "He ought, therefore, to be learned in divine law, so that he has a treasury of knowledge from which he can *bring out what is new and what is old*" (emphasis original). I am fascinated by the evenhandedness and wisdom of Benedict (and of course, of Jesus, as quoted in the Gospel of Matthew). With my engagement in public policy issues of today, and my long learning from Benedict, I see the necessity of honoring both the old and the new while discerning the best of each.
4. Norvene Vest, "Ear of the Heart," *Parabola Anthology Series*, vol. 19, no. 1 (Sandpoint, ID: Morning Light Press, 2006), 126.
5. Here and in the paragraph below: Richard Kearney, *Reimagining the Sacred* (New York: Columbia University Press, 2016), 14. Note that Mary is often depicted as reading at a sort of lectern at the moment of the Annunciation.
6. Michel Philibert, "Philosophical Imagination: Paul Ricoeur as the Singer of Ruins," in *The Philosophy of Paul Ricoeur*, Library of Living Philosophers XXII, ed. Lewis Edwin Hahn (Chicago: Open Court, 1995), 130.
7. Norvene Vest, *Re-Visioning Theology: A Mythic Approach to Religion* (Mahwah, NJ: Paulist Press, 2011), 60, 111.
8. David Stewart, "Ricoeur on Religious Language," in *Philosophy of Paul Ricoeur*, 428–29.
9. C. S. Lewis, *The Weight of Glory* (New York: Macmillan, 1949), 8–9.
10. Abraham J. Heschel, *The Prophets* (New York: Harper, 1962), 25.
11. Heschel, *Prophets*, 27; emphasis added.
12. Please note: I speak of the tradition I know best. I am aware, however, that some of these ideas, phrased differently, are characteristic of other religious traditions as well.
13. Bonnie Thurston, *O Taste and See* (Brewster, MA: Paraclete Press, 2014), 13.
14. Susan A. Muto and Adrian van Kaam, "Preface," *Am I Living a Spiritual Life?* (Denville, NJ: Dimension Books, 1978). Similar thoughts

are also found in Frederick Buechner, *The Alphabet of Grace* (San Francisco: HarperCollins, 2009).

15. Joan Chittister, Plenary Presentation at Spiritual Directors' International Conference, "Renaissance 2021," April 22, 2021.

16. Note: I encourage you to read the complete Rule in its relative smallness; if you need a little help with a sixth-century document, try the recently published inclusive translation and commentary, *St. Benedict's Rule*, by Judith Sutera, OSB (Collegeville, MN: Liturgical Press, 2021) and/or my devotional commentary *Preferring Christ: A Devotional Commentary on the Rule of St. Benedict* (New York: Morehouse Publishing, 1995).

17. We tend to continue using the Latin term because the literal English translation does not convey the nuances important for understanding its full meaning.

18. Susan A. Muto, *A Practical Guide to Spiritual Reading*, rev. ed. (Petersham, MA: St. Bede's Publications, 1994), 3.

19. Guigo II the Carthusian, "On the Purpose and Effects of Lectio Divina," *The Ladder of Monks*, vol. 48, Cistercian Studies Series, trans. E. Colledge (Kalamazoo, MI: Cistercian Publications, 1981), 73–74.

20. Two of my books discuss *lectio* in more detail: *Gathered in the Word: Praying the Scripture in Small Groups* (Nashville: Upper Room Books, 1996) and *No Moment Too Small: Rhythms of Silence, Prayer, and Holy Reading* (Kalamazoo, MI: Cistercian Publications, in cooperation with Boston: Cowley Publications, 1994).

21. Carl McColman, *The Big Book of Christian Mysticism* (Charlottesville, VA: Hampton Roads Publishing, 2010), 192–93.

22. Michael Casey, OCSO, *Coenobium: Reflections on Monastic Community*, Monastic Wisdom Series (Collegeville, MN: Cistercian Publications, 2021), 22.

23. For more detail on Evagrius's and Cassian's discussions on what might be called failures of love—that is, excessive love (unregulated desire), defective love (unregulated will), and perverted love (unregulated intellect)—see chap. 7, on virtue, in my book, *What Is Your Practice? Lifelong Growth in the Spirit*, written with the Rev. Liz Forney (New York: Morehouse Publishing, 2015), especially the chart on p. 101. Also see Mary Margaret Funk, OSB, *Thoughts Matter: The Practice of the Spiritual Life* (New York: Continuum, 1998).

24. For more reflection on this possibility, see Charles Mathewes, *A Theology of Public Life*, Cambridge Studies in Christian Doctrine (Cambridge, UK: Cambridge University Press, 2007).

25. Mathewes, *Theology of Public Life*, 8–13.

26. Kin-dom is a term introduced by Mujerista theologian Ada Maria Isasi-Diaz in *Mujerista Theology: A Theology for the 21st Century* (Maryknoll,

NY: Orbis Books, 1996) reflecting that, since we share the spark of the sacred in our humanity, we are kin in Christ.

27. Mathewes, *Theology of Public Life*, 107–10.

28. Rowan Williams, speech given at the Trinity Institute, Trinity Church, NY (2003).

29. Richard Rohr, *The Divine Dance: The Trinity and Your Transformation*, with Mike Morrell (New Kensington, PA: Whitaker House, 2016); and Elizabeth A. Johnson, *She Who Is: The Mystery of God in Feminist Theological Discourse* (New York: Crossroad, 1993).

30. Rohr, *Divine Dance*, 46–47.

31. Casey, *Coenobium*, 1.

32. Casey, 146.

33. Casey, 184.

34. Quoted in Casey, *Coenobium*, 188, from Eva Carlotta Rava, *Caída del hombre y retorna a la verdad en los primeros tratados de San Bernardo de Claraval* (Buenos Aires: EDUCA, 1986), 105. (In English, these observations are taken from a close reading of Bernard of Clairvaux's Sermon on the Feast of Saints Peter and Paul.)

35. Casey, *Coenobium*, 192.

36. Definition from the APA online *Dictionary of Psychology*.

37. Richard Rohr, *Breathing Under Water: Spirituality and the Twelve Steps* (Cincinnati, OH: Franciscan Media, 2011), xxiii.

38. Quotations in this paragraph are all from Matthew Vega, "The Geography of Whiteness," interview of Willie Jennings, *Christian Century* 138, no. 22, November 3, 2021, pp. 24–27. Jennings goes on to explain this theory in considerable detail and with considerable strength. Each of us must deal with possibility of severe distortion in Christianity as we see fit; for me, it is not by any means a call to abandon Christianity (God is certainly More than the form of a religion), but rather to reform it, as Christians have done often over the centuries. For further consideration, Jennings's most recent book is *After Whiteness: An Education in Belonging* (Grand Rapids, MI: Eerdmans, 2020). The Eerdmans webpage reports about this book: "Theological education has always been about formation: first of people, then of communities, then of the world. If we continue to promote whiteness and its related ideas of masculinity and individualism in our educational work, it will remain diseased and thwart our efforts to heal the church and the world. But if theological education aims to form people who can gather others together through border-crossing pluralism and God-drenched communion, we can begin to cultivate the radical belonging that is at the heart of God's transformative work. In this inaugural volume of the Theological Education between the Times series, Willie James Jennings shares the insights gained from his extensive experience in theological education, most notably as the

dean of a major university's divinity school—where he remains one of the only African Americans to have ever served in that role. He reflects on the distortions hidden in plain sight within the world of education but holds onto abundant hope for what theological education can be" (https://www.eerdmans.com/Products/7844/after-whiteness.aspx).

39. Willie Jennings, "The Place of Race," *Sojourners*, November 3, 2021, p. 25; emphasis added.

40. Jennings, *After Whiteness*.

41. Rowan Williams, *The Way of St. Benedict* (London: Bloomsbury Continuum, 2020), 80.

42. Raimundo Panikkar, *Blessed Simplicity: The Monk as Universal Archetype* (New York: Seabury Press, 1982), 34.

43. David Bohm, *On Dialogue*, ed. Lee Nichol (New York: Routledge, 1996).

44. Calvert Watkins, ed., *The American Heritage Dictionary of Indo-European Roots* (Boston: Houghton Mifflin, 1985).

45. William Franke, *Dante's Interpretive Journey* (Chicago: University of Chicago Press, 1996), 20.

46. David Tracy, *The Analogical Imagination: Christian Theology and the Culture of Pluralism* (New York: Crossroad, 1981), 119; emphasis added.

47. This quotation from Einstein was cited in a 2021 newsletter of St. Placid Priory, Lacey, WA.

48. Hans Urs von Balthasar, *The Glory of the Lord: A Theological Aesthetics I: Seeing the Form*, trans. Erasmo Leiva-Merikakis (San Francisco: Ignatius Press, 2009), 122.

49. Thomas Berry, *The Great Work: Our Way into the Future* (New York: Three Rivers Press, 1999), 49.